Date

Conditions

Weather

Terrain

Food Inventory

Rations ☐

Water ☐

Hunting ☐

Fishing ☐

Foraging ☐

Journey

Distance Covered

Trail Markers Used

Landmarks Sighted

Animal Prints

Shelter

Shelter Constructed ☐

Type of Shelter

Clothing/Coverings ☐

Waterproof ☐

Animal proof ☐

Sunproof ☐

Fire Started ☐

Map Sketch

Lat. Long.

Party Member	Status	Injuries	Treatment

Date ____________

Conditions

Weather

Terrain

Shelter

Shelter Constructed ☐

Type of Shelter

Clothing/Coverings ☐

Waterproof ☐

Animal proof ☐

Sunproof ☐

Fire Started ☐

Food Inventory

Rations ☐

Water ☐

Hunting ☐

Fishing ☐

Foraging ☐

Journey

Distance Covered

Trail Markers Used

Landmarks Sighted

Animal Prints

Map Sketch

Lat. Long.

Party Member	Status	Injuries	Treatment

Date

Conditions

Weather

Terrain

Shelter

Shelter Constructed ☐

Type of Shelter

Clothing/Coverings ☐

Waterproof ☐

Animal proof ☐

Sunproof ☐

Fire Started ☐

Food Inventory

Rations ☐

Water ☐

Hunting ☐

Fishing ☐

Foraging ☐

Journey

Distance Covered

Trail Markers Used

Landmarks Sighted

Animal Prints

Map Sketch

Lat. Long.

Party Member	Status	Injuries	Treatment

Date

Conditions

Weather

Terrain

Shelter

Shelter Constructed ☐

Type of Shelter

Clothing/Coverings ☐

Waterproof ☐

Animal proof ☐

Sunproof ☐

Fire Started ☐

Food Inventory

Rations ☐

Water ☐

Hunting ☐

Fishing ☐

Foraging ☐

Journey

Distance Covered

Trail Markers Used

Landmarks Sighted

Animal Prints

Map Sketch

Lat. Long.

Party Member	Status	Injuries	Treatment

Date

Conditions

Weather

Terrain

Shelter

Shelter Constructed ☐

Type of Shelter

Clothing/Coverings ☐

Waterproof ☐

Animal proof ☐

Sunproof ☐

Fire Started ☐

Food Inventory

Rations ☐

Water ☐

Hunting ☐

Fishing ☐

Foraging ☐

Journey

Distance Covered

Trail Markers Used

Landmarks Sighted

Animal Prints

Map Sketch

Lat. Long.

Party Member	Status	Injuries	Treatment

Date

Conditions

Weather

Terrain

Shelter

Shelter Constructed ☐

Type of Shelter

Clothing/Coverings ☐

Waterproof ☐

Animal proof ☐

Sunproof ☐

Fire Started ☐

Food Inventory

Rations ☐

Water ☐

Hunting ☐

Fishing ☐

Foraging ☐

Journey

Distance Covered

Trail Markers Used

Landmarks Sighted

Animal Prints

Map Sketch

Lat.

Long.

Party Member	Status	Injuries	Treatment

Date

Conditions

Weather

Terrain

Shelter

Shelter Constructed ☐

Type of Shelter

Clothing/Coverings ☐

Waterproof ☐

Animal proof ☐

Sunproof ☐

Fire Started ☐

Food Inventory

Rations ☐

Water ☐

Hunting ☐

Fishing ☐

Foraging ☐

Journey

Distance Covered

Trail Markers Used

Landmarks Sighted

Animal Prints

Map Sketch

Lat. Long.

Party Member	Status	Injuries	Treatment

Date

Conditions

Weather

Terrain

Shelter

Shelter Constructed ☐

Type of Shelter

Clothing/Coverings ☐

Waterproof ☐

Animal proof ☐

Sunproof ☐

Fire Started ☐

Food Inventory

Rations ☐

Water ☐

Hunting ☐

Fishing ☐

Foraging ☐

Journey

Distance Covered

Trail Markers Used

Landmarks Sighted

Animal Prints

Map Sketch

Lat. Long.

Party Member	Status	Injuries	Treatment

Date ____________

Conditions

Weather

Terrain

Shelter

Shelter Constructed ☐

Type of Shelter

Clothing/Coverings ☐

Waterproof ☐

Animal proof ☐

Sunproof ☐

Fire Started ☐

Food Inventory

Rations ☐

Water ☐

Hunting ☐

Fishing ☐

Foraging ☐

Journey

Distance Covered

Trail Markers Used

Landmarks Sighted

Animal Prints

Map Sketch

Lat. Long.

Party Member	Status	Injuries	Treatment

Date

Conditions

Weather

Terrain

Shelter

Shelter Constructed ☐

Type of Shelter

Clothing/Coverings ☐

Waterproof ☐

Animal proof ☐

Sunproof ☐

Fire Started ☐

Food Inventory

Rations ☐

Water ☐

Hunting ☐

Fishing ☐

Foraging ☐

Journey

Distance Covered

Trail Markers Used

Landmarks Sighted

Animal Prints

Map Sketch

Lat. Long.

Party Member	Status	Injuries	Treatment

Date ____________

Conditions

Weather

Terrain

Food Inventory

Rations ☐

Water ☐

Hunting ☐

Fishing ☐

Foraging ☐

Journey

Distance Covered

Trail Markers Used

Landmarks Sighted

Animal Prints

Shelter

Shelter Constructed ☐

Type of Shelter

Clothing/Coverings ☐

Waterproof ☐

Animal proof ☐

Sunproof ☐

Fire Started ☐

Map Sketch

Lat.

Long.

Party Member	Status	Injuries	Treatment

Date ______________

Conditions

Weather

Terrain

Shelter

Shelter Constructed ☐

Type of Shelter

____

____

____

Clothing/Coverings ☐

Waterproof ☐

Animal proof ☐

Sunproof ☐

Fire Started ☐

Food Inventory

Rations ☐

____

____

____

____

Water ☐

Hunting ☐

____

____

____

Fishing ☐

____

____

____

Foraging ☐

____

____

____

Journey

Distance Covered

Trail Markers Used

Landmarks Sighted

Animal Prints

Map Sketch

Lat. Long.

Party Member	Status	Injuries	Treatment

Date ____________

Conditions

Weather

Terrain

Shelter

Shelter Constructed ☐

Type of Shelter

Clothing/Coverings ☐

Waterproof ☐

Animal proof ☐

Sunproof ☐

Fire Started ☐

Food Inventory

Rations ☐

Water ☐

Hunting ☐

Fishing ☐

Foraging ☐

Journey

Distance Covered

Trail Markers Used

Landmarks Sighted

Animal Prints

Map Sketch

Lat. Long.

Party Member	Status	Injuries	Treatment

Date

Conditions

Weather

Terrain

Shelter

Shelter Constructed ☐

Type of Shelter

Clothing/Coverings ☐

Waterproof ☐

Animal proof ☐

Sunproof ☐

Fire Started ☐

Food Inventory

Rations ☐

Water ☐

Hunting ☐

Fishing ☐

Foraging ☐

Journey

Distance Covered

Trail Markers Used

Landmarks Sighted

Animal Prints

Map Sketch

Lat. Long.

Party Member	Status	Injuries	Treatment

Date

Conditions

Weather

Terrain

Shelter

Shelter Constructed ☐

Type of Shelter

Clothing/Coverings ☐

Waterproof ☐

Animal proof ☐

Sunproof ☐

Fire Started ☐

Food Inventory

Rations ☐

Water ☐

Hunting ☐

Fishing ☐

Foraging ☐

Journey

Distance Covered

Trail Markers Used

Landmarks Sighted

Animal Prints

Map Sketch

Lat. Long.

Party Member	Status	Injuries	Treatment

Date

Conditions

Weather

Terrain

Shelter

Shelter Constructed ☐

Type of Shelter

Clothing/Coverings ☐

Waterproof ☐

Animal proof ☐

Sunproof ☐

Fire Started ☐

Food Inventory

Rations ☐

Water ☐

Hunting ☐

Fishing ☐

Foraging ☐

Journey

Distance Covered

Trail Markers Used

Landmarks Sighted

Animal Prints

Map Sketch

Lat. Long.

Party Member	Status	Injuries	Treatment

Date

Conditions

Weather

Terrain

Shelter

Shelter Constructed ☐

Type of Shelter

Clothing/Coverings ☐

Waterproof ☐

Animal proof ☐

Sunproof ☐

Fire Started ☐

Food Inventory

Rations ☐

Water ☐

Hunting ☐

Fishing ☐

Foraging ☐

Journey

Distance Covered

Trail Markers Used

Landmarks Sighted

Animal Prints

Map Sketch

Lat. Long.

Party Member	Status	Injuries	Treatment

Date

Conditions

Weather

Terrain

Shelter

Shelter Constructed ☐

Type of Shelter

Clothing/Coverings ☐

Waterproof ☐

Animal proof ☐

Sunproof ☐

Fire Started ☐

Food Inventory

Rations ☐

Water ☐

Hunting ☐

Fishing ☐

Foraging ☐

Journey

Distance Covered

Trail Markers Used

Landmarks Sighted

Animal Prints

Map Sketch

Lat. Long.

Party Member	Status	Injuries	Treatment

Date

Conditions

Weather

Terrain

Shelter

Shelter Constructed ☐

Type of Shelter

Clothing/Coverings ☐

Waterproof ☐

Animal proof ☐

Sunproof ☐

Fire Started ☐

Food Inventory

Rations ☐

Water ☐

Hunting ☐

Fishing ☐

Foraging ☐

Journey

Distance Covered

Trail Markers Used

Landmarks Sighted

Animal Prints

Map Sketch

Lat.

Long.

Party Member	Status	Injuries	Treatment

Date ____________

Conditions

Weather

Terrain

Shelter

Shelter Constructed ☐

Type of Shelter

Clothing/Coverings ☐

Waterproof ☐

Animal proof ☐

Sunproof ☐

Fire Started ☐

Food Inventory

Rations ☐

Water ☐

Hunting ☐

Fishing ☐

Foraging ☐

Journey

Distance Covered

Trail Markers Used

Landmarks Sighted

Animal Prints

Map Sketch

Lat. Long.

Party Member	Status	Injuries	Treatment

Date

Conditions

Weather

Terrain

Shelter

Shelter Constructed ☐

Type of Shelter

Clothing/Coverings ☐

Waterproof ☐

Animal proof ☐

Sunproof ☐

Fire Started ☐

Food Inventory

Rations ☐

Water ☐

Hunting ☐

Fishing ☐

Foraging ☐

Journey

Distance Covered

Trail Markers Used

Landmarks Sighted

Animal Prints

Map Sketch

Lat. Long.

Party Member	Status	Injuries	Treatment

Date ______

Conditions

Weather

Terrain

Food Inventory

Rations ☐

Water ☐

Hunting ☐

Fishing ☐

Foraging ☐

Journey

Distance Covered

Trail Markers Used

Landmarks Sighted

Animal Prints

Shelter

Shelter Constructed ☐

Type of Shelter

Clothing/Coverings ☐

Waterproof ☐

Animal proof ☐

Sunproof ☐

Fire Started ☐

Map Sketch

Lat. Long.

Party Member	Status	Injuries	Treatment

Date

Conditions

Weather

Terrain

Food Inventory

Rations ☐

Water ☐

Hunting ☐

Fishing ☐

Foraging ☐

Journey

Distance Covered

Trail Markers Used

Landmarks Sighted

Animal Prints

Shelter

Shelter Constructed ☐

Type of Shelter

Clothing/Coverings ☐

Waterproof ☐

Animal proof ☐

Sunproof ☐

Fire Started ☐

Map Sketch

Lat. Long.

Party Member	Status	Injuries	Treatment

Date

Conditions

Weather

Terrain

Shelter

Shelter Constructed ☐

Type of Shelter

Clothing/Coverings ☐

Waterproof ☐

Animal proof ☐

Sunproof ☐

Fire Started ☐

Food Inventory

Rations ☐

Water ☐

Hunting ☐

Fishing ☐

Foraging ☐

Journey

Distance Covered

Trail Markers Used

Landmarks Sighted

Animal Prints

Map Sketch

Lat. Long.

Party Member	Status	Injuries	Treatment

Date

Conditions

Weather

Terrain

Shelter

Shelter Constructed ☐

Type of Shelter

Clothing/Coverings ☐

Waterproof ☐

Animal proof ☐

Sunproof ☐

Fire Started ☐

Food Inventory

Rations ☐

Water ☐

Hunting ☐

Fishing ☐

Foraging ☐

Journey

Distance Covered

Trail Markers Used

Landmarks Sighted

Animal Prints

Map Sketch

Lat. Long.

Party Member	Status	Injuries	Treatment

Date

Conditions

Weather

Terrain

Shelter

Shelter Constructed ☐

Type of Shelter

Clothing/Coverings ☐

Waterproof ☐

Animal proof ☐

Sunproof ☐

Fire Started ☐

Food Inventory

Rations ☐

Water ☐

Hunting ☐

Fishing ☐

Foraging ☐

Journey

Distance Covered

Trail Markers Used

Landmarks Sighted

Animal Prints

Map Sketch

Lat. Long.

Party Member	Status	Injuries	Treatment

Date

Conditions

Weather

Terrain

Shelter

Shelter Constructed ☐

Type of Shelter

Clothing/Coverings ☐

Waterproof ☐

Animal proof ☐

Sunproof ☐

Fire Started ☐

Food Inventory

Rations ☐

Water ☐

Hunting ☐

Fishing ☐

Foraging ☐

Journey

Distance Covered

Trail Markers Used

Landmarks Sighted

Animal Prints

Map Sketch

Lat.

Long.

Party Member	Status	Injuries	Treatment

Date

Conditions

Weather

Terrain

Shelter

Shelter Constructed ☐

Type of Shelter

Clothing/Coverings ☐

Waterproof ☐

Animal proof ☐

Sunproof ☐

Fire Started ☐

Food Inventory

Rations ☐

Water ☐

Hunting ☐

Fishing ☐

Foraging ☐

Journey

Distance Covered

Trail Markers Used

Landmarks Sighted

Animal Prints

Map Sketch

Lat.

Long.

Party Member	Status	Injuries	Treatment

Date

Conditions

Weather

Terrain

Shelter

Shelter Constructed ☐

Type of Shelter

Clothing/Coverings ☐

Waterproof ☐

Animal proof ☐

Sunproof ☐

Fire Started ☐

Food Inventory

Rations ☐

Water ☐

Hunting ☐

Fishing ☐

Foraging ☐

Journey

Distance Covered

Trail Markers Used

Landmarks Sighted

Animal Prints

Map Sketch

Lat.

Long.

Party Member	Status	Injuries	Treatment

Date ____________

Conditions

Weather

Terrain

Shelter

Shelter Constructed ☐

Type of Shelter

Clothing/Coverings ☐

Waterproof ☐

Animal proof ☐

Sunproof ☐

Fire Started ☐

Food Inventory

Rations ☐

Water ☐

Hunting ☐

Fishing ☐

Foraging ☐

Journey

Distance Covered

Trail Markers Used

Landmarks Sighted

Animal Prints

Map Sketch

Lat. Long.

Party Member	Status	Injuries	Treatment

Date

Conditions

Weather

Terrain

Shelter

Shelter Constructed ☐

Type of Shelter

Clothing/Coverings ☐

Waterproof ☐

Animal proof ☐

Sunproof ☐

Fire Started ☐

Food Inventory

Rations ☐

Water ☐

Hunting ☐

Fishing ☐

Foraging ☐

Journey

Distance Covered

Trail Markers Used

Landmarks Sighted

Animal Prints

Map Sketch

Lat.

Long.

Party Member	Status	Injuries	Treatment

Date

Conditions

Weather

Terrain

Shelter

Shelter Constructed ☐

Type of Shelter

Clothing/Coverings ☐

Waterproof ☐

Animal proof ☐

Sunproof ☐

Fire Started ☐

Food Inventory

Rations ☐

Water ☐

Hunting ☐

Fishing ☐

Foraging ☐

Journey

Distance Covered

Trail Markers Used

Landmarks Sighted

Animal Prints

Map Sketch

Lat.

Long.

Party Member	Status	Injuries	Treatment

Date

Conditions

Weather

Terrain

Shelter

Shelter Constructed ☐

Type of Shelter

Clothing/Coverings ☐

Waterproof ☐

Animal proof ☐

Sunproof ☐

Fire Started ☐

Food Inventory

Rations ☐

Water ☐

Hunting ☐

Fishing ☐

Foraging ☐

Journey

Distance Covered

Trail Markers Used

Landmarks Sighted

Animal Prints

Map Sketch

Lat. Long.

Party Member	Status	Injuries	Treatment

Date

Conditions

Weather

Terrain

Food Inventory

Rations ☐

Water ☐

Hunting ☐

Fishing ☐

Foraging ☐

Journey

Distance Covered

Trail Markers Used

Landmarks Sighted

Animal Prints

Shelter

Shelter Constructed ☐

Type of Shelter

Clothing/Coverings ☐

Waterproof ☐

Animal proof ☐

Sunproof ☐

Fire Started ☐

Map Sketch

Lat. Long.

Party Member	Status	Injuries	Treatment

Date

Conditions

Weather

Terrain

Shelter

Shelter Constructed ☐

Type of Shelter

Clothing/Coverings ☐

Waterproof ☐

Animal proof ☐

Sunproof ☐

Fire Started ☐

Food Inventory

Rations ☐

Water ☐

Hunting ☐

Fishing ☐

Foraging ☐

Journey

Distance Covered

Trail Markers Used

Landmarks Sighted

Animal Prints

Map Sketch

Lat.

Long.

Party Member	Status	Injuries	Treatment

Date ____________

Conditions

Weather

Terrain

Food Inventory

Rations ☐

Water ☐

Hunting ☐

Fishing ☐

Foraging ☐

Journey

Distance Covered

Trail Markers Used

Landmarks Sighted

Animal Prints

Shelter

Shelter Constructed ☐

Type of Shelter

Clothing/Coverings ☐

Waterproof ☐

Animal proof ☐

Sunproof ☐

Fire Started ☐

Map Sketch

Lat. Long.

Party Member	Status	Injuries	Treatment

Date ____________

Conditions

Weather

Terrain

Shelter

Shelter Constructed ☐

Type of Shelter

Clothing/Coverings ☐

Waterproof ☐

Animal proof ☐

Sunproof ☐

Fire Started ☐

Food Inventory

Rations ☐

Water ☐

Hunting ☐

Fishing ☐

Foraging ☐

Journey

Distance Covered

Trail Markers Used

Landmarks Sighted

Animal Prints

Map Sketch

Lat. Long.

Party Member	Status	Injuries	Treatment

Date

Conditions

Weather

Terrain

Shelter

Shelter Constructed ☐

Type of Shelter

Clothing/Coverings ☐

Waterproof ☐

Animal proof ☐

Sunproof ☐

Fire Started ☐

Food Inventory

Rations ☐

Water ☐

Hunting ☐

Fishing ☐

Foraging ☐

Journey

Distance Covered

Trail Markers Used

Landmarks Sighted

Animal Prints

Map Sketch

Lat. Long.

Party Member	Status	Injuries	Treatment

Date

Conditions

Weather

Terrain

Food Inventory

Rations ☐

Water ☐

Hunting ☐

Fishing ☐

Foraging ☐

Journey

Distance Covered

Trail Markers Used

Landmarks Sighted

Animal Prints

Shelter

Shelter Constructed ☐

Type of Shelter

Clothing/Coverings ☐

Waterproof ☐

Animal proof ☐

Sunproof ☐

Fire Started ☐

Map Sketch

Lat. Long.

Party Member	Status	Injuries	Treatment

Date

Conditions

Weather

Terrain

Shelter

Shelter Constructed ☐

Type of Shelter

Clothing/Coverings ☐

Waterproof ☐

Animal proof ☐

Sunproof ☐

Fire Started ☐

Food Inventory

Rations ☐

Water ☐

Hunting ☐

Fishing ☐

Foraging ☐

Journey

Distance Covered

Trail Markers Used

Landmarks Sighted

Animal Prints

Map Sketch

Lat. Long.

Party Member	Status	Injuries	Treatment

Date ____________

Conditions

Weather

Terrain

Shelter

Shelter Constructed ☐

Type of Shelter

Clothing/Coverings ☐

Waterproof ☐

Animal proof ☐

Sunproof ☐

Fire Started ☐

Food Inventory

Rations ☐

Water ☐

Hunting ☐

Fishing ☐

Foraging ☐

Journey

Distance Covered

Trail Markers Used

Landmarks Sighted

Animal Prints

Map Sketch

Lat. Long.

Party Member	Status	Injuries	Treatment

Date

Conditions

Weather

Terrain

Shelter

Shelter Constructed ☐

Type of Shelter

Clothing/Coverings ☐

Waterproof ☐

Animal proof ☐

Sunproof ☐

Fire Started ☐

Food Inventory

Rations ☐

Water ☐

Hunting ☐

Fishing ☐

Foraging ☐

Journey

Distance Covered

Trail Markers Used

Landmarks Sighted

Animal Prints

Map Sketch

Lat.

Long.

Party Member	Status	Injuries	Treatment

Date ____________

Conditions

Weather

Terrain

Shelter

Shelter Constructed ☐

Type of Shelter

Clothing/Coverings ☐

Waterproof ☐

Animal proof ☐

Sunproof ☐

Fire Started ☐

Food Inventory

Rations ☐

Water ☐

Hunting ☐

Fishing ☐

Foraging ☐

Journey

Distance Covered

Trail Markers Used

Landmarks Sighted

Animal Prints

Map Sketch

Lat. Long.

Party Member	Status	Injuries	Treatment

Date

Conditions

Weather

Terrain

Shelter

Shelter Constructed ☐

Type of Shelter

Clothing/Coverings ☐

Waterproof ☐

Animal proof ☐

Sunproof ☐

Fire Started ☐

Food Inventory

Rations ☐

Water ☐

Hunting ☐

Fishing ☐

Foraging ☐

Journey

Distance Covered

Trail Markers Used

Landmarks Sighted

Animal Prints

Map Sketch

Lat.

Long.

Party Member	Status	Injuries	Treatment

Date

Conditions

Weather

Terrain

Shelter

Shelter Constructed ☐

Type of Shelter

Clothing/Coverings ☐

Waterproof ☐

Animal proof ☐

Sunproof ☐

Fire Started ☐

Food Inventory

Rations ☐

Water ☐

Hunting ☐

Fishing ☐

Foraging ☐

Journey

Distance Covered

Trail Markers Used

Landmarks Sighted

Animal Prints

Map Sketch

Lat. Long.

Party Member	Status	Injuries	Treatment

Date

Conditions

Weather

Terrain

Shelter

Shelter Constructed ☐

Type of Shelter

Clothing/Coverings ☐

Waterproof ☐

Animal proof ☐

Sunproof ☐

Fire Started ☐

Food Inventory

Rations ☐

Water ☐

Hunting ☐

Fishing ☐

Foraging ☐

Journey

Distance Covered

Trail Markers Used

Landmarks Sighted

Animal Prints

Map Sketch

Lat. Long.

Party Member	Status	Injuries	Treatment

Date

Conditions

Weather

Terrain

Shelter

Shelter Constructed ☐

Type of Shelter

Clothing/Coverings ☐

Waterproof ☐

Animal proof ☐

Sunproof ☐

Fire Started ☐

Food Inventory

Rations ☐

Water ☐

Hunting ☐

Fishing ☐

Foraging ☐

Journey

Distance Covered

Trail Markers Used

Landmarks Sighted

Animal Prints

Map Sketch

Lat. Long.

Party Member	Status	Injuries	Treatment

Date

Conditions

Weather

Terrain

Shelter

Shelter Constructed ☐

Type of Shelter

Clothing/Coverings ☐

Waterproof ☐

Animal proof ☐

Sunproof ☐

Fire Started ☐

Food Inventory

Rations ☐

Water ☐

Hunting ☐

Fishing ☐

Foraging ☐

Journey

Distance Covered

Trail Markers Used

Landmarks Sighted

Animal Prints

Map Sketch

Lat. Long.

Party Member	Status	Injuries	Treatment

Date

Conditions

Weather

Terrain

Food Inventory

Rations ☐

Water ☐

Hunting ☐

Fishing ☐

Foraging ☐

Journey

Distance Covered

Trail Markers Used

Landmarks Sighted

Animal Prints

Shelter

Shelter Constructed ☐

Type of Shelter

Clothing/Coverings ☐

Waterproof ☐

Animal proof ☐

Sunproof ☐

Fire Started ☐

Map Sketch

Lat.

Long.

Party Member	Status	Injuries	Treatment

Date

Conditions

Weather

Terrain

Shelter

Shelter Constructed ☐

Type of Shelter

Clothing/Coverings ☐

Waterproof ☐

Animal proof ☐

Sunproof ☐

Fire Started ☐

Food Inventory

Rations ☐

Water ☐

Hunting ☐

Fishing ☐

Foraging ☐

Journey

Distance Covered

Trail Markers Used

Landmarks Sighted

Animal Prints

Map Sketch

Lat. Long.

Party Member	Status	Injuries	Treatment

Date ____________

Conditions

Weather

Terrain

Shelter

Shelter Constructed ☐

Type of Shelter

Clothing/Coverings ☐

Waterproof ☐

Animal proof ☐

Sunproof ☐

Fire Started ☐

Food Inventory

Rations ☐

Water ☐

Hunting ☐

Fishing ☐

Foraging ☐

Journey

Distance Covered

Trail Markers Used

Landmarks Sighted

Animal Prints

Map Sketch

Lat. Long.

Party Member	Status	Injuries	Treatment

Date

Conditions

Weather

Terrain

Shelter

Shelter Constructed ☐

Type of Shelter

Clothing/Coverings ☐

Waterproof ☐

Animal proof ☐

Sunproof ☐

Fire Started ☐

Food Inventory

Rations ☐

Water ☐

Hunting ☐

Fishing ☐

Foraging ☐

Journey

Distance Covered

Trail Markers Used

Landmarks Sighted

Animal Prints

Map Sketch

Lat. Long.

Party Member	Status	Injuries	Treatment

Date ____________

Conditions

Weather

Terrain

Shelter

Shelter Constructed ☐

Type of Shelter

Clothing/Coverings ☐

Waterproof ☐

Animal proof ☐

Sunproof ☐

Fire Started ☐

Food Inventory

Rations ☐

Water ☐

Hunting ☐

Fishing ☐

Foraging ☐

Journey

Distance Covered

Trail Markers Used

Landmarks Sighted

Animal Prints

Map Sketch

Lat. Long.

Party Member	Status	Injuries	Treatment

Date

Conditions

Weather

Terrain

Shelter

Shelter Constructed ☐

Type of Shelter

Clothing/Coverings ☐

Waterproof ☐

Animal proof ☐

Sunproof ☐

Fire Started ☐

Food Inventory

Rations ☐

Water ☐

Hunting ☐

Fishing ☐

Foraging ☐

Journey

Distance Covered

Trail Markers Used

Landmarks Sighted

Animal Prints

Map Sketch

Lat. Long.

Party Member	Status	Injuries	Treatment

Date ____________

Conditions

Weather

Terrain

Food Inventory

Rations ☐

Water ☐

Hunting ☐

Fishing ☐

Foraging ☐

Journey

Distance Covered

Trail Markers Used

Landmarks Sighted

Animal Prints

Shelter

Shelter Constructed ☐

Type of Shelter

Clothing/Coverings ☐

Waterproof ☐

Animal proof ☐

Sunproof ☐

Fire Started ☐

Map Sketch

Lat. Long.

Party Member	Status	Injuries	Treatment

Date ____________

Conditions

Weather

Terrain

Shelter

Shelter Constructed ☐

Type of Shelter

Clothing/Coverings ☐

Waterproof ☐

Animal proof ☐

Sunproof ☐

Fire Started ☐

Food Inventory

Rations ☐

Water ☐

Hunting ☐

Fishing ☐

Foraging ☐

Journey

Distance Covered

Trail Markers Used

Landmarks Sighted

Animal Prints

Map Sketch

Lat.

Long.

Party Member	Status	Injuries	Treatment

Date ______________

Conditions

Weather

Terrain

Shelter

Shelter Constructed ☐

Type of Shelter

Clothing/Coverings ☐

Waterproof ☐

Animal proof ☐

Sunproof ☐

Fire Started ☐

Food Inventory

Rations ☐

Water ☐

Hunting ☐

Fishing ☐

Foraging ☐

Journey

Distance Covered

Trail Markers Used

Landmarks Sighted

Animal Prints

Map Sketch

Lat.

Long.

Party Member	Status	Injuries	Treatment

Date

Conditions

Weather

Terrain

Food Inventory

Rations ☐

Water ☐

Hunting ☐

Fishing ☐

Foraging ☐

Journey

Distance Covered

Trail Markers Used

Landmarks Sighted

Animal Prints

Shelter

Shelter Constructed ☐

Type of Shelter

Clothing/Coverings ☐

Waterproof ☐

Animal proof ☐

Sunproof ☐

Fire Started ☐

Map Sketch

Lat. Long.

Party Member	Status	Injuries	Treatment

Date

Conditions

Weather

Terrain

Shelter

Shelter Constructed ☐

Type of Shelter

Clothing/Coverings ☐

Waterproof ☐

Animal proof ☐

Sunproof ☐

Fire Started ☐

Food Inventory

Rations ☐

Water ☐

Hunting ☐

Fishing ☐

Foraging ☐

Journey

Distance Covered

Trail Markers Used

Landmarks Sighted

Animal Prints

Map Sketch

Lat. Long.

Party Member	Status	Injuries	Treatment

Date

Conditions

Weather

Terrain

Shelter

Shelter Constructed ☐

Type of Shelter

Clothing/Coverings ☐

Waterproof ☐

Animal proof ☐

Sunproof ☐

Fire Started ☐

Food Inventory

Rations ☐

Water ☐

Hunting ☐

Fishing ☐

Foraging ☐

Journey

Distance Covered

Trail Markers Used

Landmarks Sighted

Animal Prints

Map Sketch

Lat. Long.

Party Member	Status	Injuries	Treatment

Date

Conditions

Weather

Terrain

Shelter

Shelter Constructed ☐

Type of Shelter

Clothing/Coverings ☐

Waterproof ☐

Animal proof ☐

Sunproof ☐

Fire Started ☐

Food Inventory

Rations ☐

Water ☐

Hunting ☐

Fishing ☐

Foraging ☐

Journey

Distance Covered

Trail Markers Used

Landmarks Sighted

Animal Prints

Map Sketch

Lat. Long.

Party Member	Status	Injuries	Treatment

Date ______

Conditions

Weather

Terrain

Food Inventory

Rations ☐

Water ☐

Hunting ☐

Fishing ☐

Foraging ☐

Journey

Distance Covered

Trail Markers Used

Landmarks Sighted

Animal Prints

Shelter

Shelter Constructed ☐

Type of Shelter

Clothing/Coverings ☐

Waterproof ☐

Animal proof ☐

Sunproof ☐

Fire Started ☐

Map Sketch

Lat. Long.

Party Member	Status	Injuries	Treatment

Date

Conditions

Weather

Terrain

Shelter

Shelter Constructed ☐

Type of Shelter

Clothing/Coverings ☐

Waterproof ☐

Animal proof ☐

Sunproof ☐

Fire Started ☐

Food Inventory

Rations ☐

Water ☐

Hunting ☐

Fishing ☐

Foraging ☐

Journey

Distance Covered

Trail Markers Used

Landmarks Sighted

Animal Prints

Map Sketch

Lat. Long.

Party Member	Status	Injuries	Treatment

Date

Conditions

Weather

Terrain

Shelter

Shelter Constructed ☐

Type of Shelter

Clothing/Coverings ☐

Waterproof ☐

Animal proof ☐

Sunproof ☐

Fire Started ☐

Food Inventory

Rations ☐

Water ☐

Hunting ☐

Fishing ☐

Foraging ☐

Journey

Distance Covered

Trail Markers Used

Landmarks Sighted

Animal Prints

Map Sketch

Lat. Long.

Party Member	Status	Injuries	Treatment

Date

Conditions

Weather

Terrain

Shelter

Shelter Constructed ☐

Type of Shelter

Clothing/Coverings ☐

Waterproof ☐

Animal proof ☐

Sunproof ☐

Fire Started ☐

Food Inventory

Rations ☐

Water ☐

Hunting ☐

Fishing ☐

Foraging ☐

Journey

Distance Covered

Trail Markers Used

Landmarks Sighted

Animal Prints

Map Sketch

Lat. Long.

Party Member	Status	Injuries	Treatment

Date

Conditions

Weather

Terrain

Shelter

Shelter Constructed ☐

Type of Shelter

Clothing/Coverings ☐

Waterproof ☐

Animal proof ☐

Sunproof ☐

Fire Started ☐

Food Inventory

Rations ☐

Water ☐

Hunting ☐

Fishing ☐

Foraging ☐

Journey

Distance Covered

Trail Markers Used

Landmarks Sighted

Animal Prints

Map Sketch

Lat. Long.

Party Member	Status	Injuries	Treatment

Date

Conditions

Weather

Terrain

Shelter

Shelter Constructed ☐

Type of Shelter

Clothing/Coverings ☐

Waterproof ☐

Animal proof ☐

Sunproof ☐

Fire Started ☐

Food Inventory

Rations ☐

Water ☐

Hunting ☐

Fishing ☐

Foraging ☐

Journey

Distance Covered

Trail Markers Used

Landmarks Sighted

Animal Prints

Map Sketch

Lat. Long.

Party Member	Status	Injuries	Treatment

Date

Conditions

Weather

Terrain

Shelter

Shelter Constructed ☐

Type of Shelter

Clothing/Coverings ☐

Waterproof ☐

Animal proof ☐

Sunproof ☐

Fire Started ☐

Food Inventory

Rations ☐

Water ☐

Hunting ☐

Fishing ☐

Foraging ☐

Journey

Distance Covered

Trail Markers Used

Landmarks Sighted

Animal Prints

Map Sketch

Lat. Long.

Party Member	Status	Injuries	Treatment

Date

Conditions

Weather

Terrain

Shelter

Shelter Constructed ☐

Type of Shelter

Clothing/Coverings ☐

Waterproof ☐

Animal proof ☐

Sunproof ☐

Fire Started ☐

Food Inventory

Rations ☐

Water ☐

Hunting ☐

Fishing ☐

Foraging ☐

Journey

Distance Covered

Trail Markers Used

Landmarks Sighted

Animal Prints

Map Sketch

Lat. Long.

Party Member	Status	Injuries	Treatment

Date

Conditions

Weather

Terrain

Shelter

Shelter Constructed ☐

Type of Shelter

Clothing/Coverings ☐

Waterproof ☐

Animal proof ☐

Sunproof ☐

Fire Started ☐

Food Inventory

Rations ☐

Water ☐

Hunting ☐

Fishing ☐

Foraging ☐

Journey

Distance Covered

Trail Markers Used

Landmarks Sighted

Animal Prints

Map Sketch

Lat. Long.

Party Member	Status	Injuries	Treatment

Date

Conditions

Weather

Terrain

Food Inventory

Rations ☐

Water ☐

Hunting ☐

Fishing ☐

Foraging ☐

Journey

Distance Covered

Trail Markers Used

Landmarks Sighted

Animal Prints

Shelter

Shelter Constructed ☐

Type of Shelter

Clothing/Coverings ☐

Waterproof ☐

Animal proof ☐

Sunproof ☐

Fire Started ☐

Map Sketch

Lat. Long.

Party Member	Status	Injuries	Treatment

Date ____________

Conditions

Weather

Terrain

Shelter

Shelter Constructed ☐

Type of Shelter

Clothing/Coverings ☐

Waterproof ☐

Animal proof ☐

Sunproof ☐

Fire Started ☐

Food Inventory

Rations ☐

Water ☐

Hunting ☐

Fishing ☐

Foraging ☐

Journey

Distance Covered

Trail Markers Used

Landmarks Sighted

Animal Prints

Map Sketch

Lat.

Long.

Party Member	Status	Injuries	Treatment

Date ____________

Conditions

Weather

Terrain

Shelter

Shelter Constructed ☐

Type of Shelter

Clothing/Coverings ☐

Waterproof ☐

Animal proof ☐

Sunproof ☐

Fire Started ☐

Food Inventory

Rations ☐

Water ☐

Hunting ☐

Fishing ☐

Foraging ☐

Journey

Distance Covered

Trail Markers Used

Landmarks Sighted

Animal Prints

Map Sketch

Lat. Long.

Party Member	Status	Injuries	Treatment

Date ____________

Conditions

Weather

Terrain

Food Inventory

Rations ☐

Water ☐

Hunting ☐

Fishing ☐

Foraging ☐

Journey

Distance Covered

Trail Markers Used

Landmarks Sighted

Animal Prints

Shelter

Shelter Constructed ☐

Type of Shelter

Clothing/Coverings ☐

Waterproof ☐

Animal proof ☐

Sunproof ☐

Fire Started ☐

Map Sketch

Lat.

Long.

Party Member	Status	Injuries	Treatment

Date

Conditions

Weather

Terrain

Food Inventory

Rations ☐

Water ☐

Hunting ☐

Fishing ☐

Foraging ☐

Journey

Distance Covered

Trail Markers Used

Landmarks Sighted

Animal Prints

Shelter

Shelter Constructed ☐

Type of Shelter

Clothing/Coverings ☐

Waterproof ☐

Animal proof ☐

Sunproof ☐

Fire Started ☐

Map Sketch

Lat. Long.

Party Member	Status	Injuries	Treatment

Date

Conditions

Weather

Terrain

Shelter

Shelter Constructed ☐

Type of Shelter

Clothing/Coverings ☐

Waterproof ☐

Animal proof ☐

Sunproof ☐

Fire Started ☐

Food Inventory

Rations ☐

Water ☐

Hunting ☐

Fishing ☐

Foraging ☐

Journey

Distance Covered

Trail Markers Used

Landmarks Sighted

Animal Prints

Map Sketch

Lat.

Long.

Party Member	Status	Injuries	Treatment

Date

Conditions

Weather

Terrain

Shelter

Shelter Constructed ☐

Type of Shelter

Clothing/Coverings ☐

Waterproof ☐

Animal proof ☐

Sunproof ☐

Fire Started ☐

Food Inventory

Rations ☐

Water ☐

Hunting ☐

Fishing ☐

Foraging ☐

Journey

Distance Covered

Trail Markers Used

Landmarks Sighted

Animal Prints

Map Sketch

Lat. Long.

Party Member	Status	Injuries	Treatment

Date

Conditions

Weather

Terrain

Shelter

Shelter Constructed ☐

Type of Shelter

Clothing/Coverings ☐

Waterproof ☐

Animal proof ☐

Sunproof ☐

Fire Started ☐

Food Inventory

Rations ☐

Water ☐

Hunting ☐

Fishing ☐

Foraging ☐

Journey

Distance Covered

Trail Markers Used

Landmarks Sighted

Animal Prints

Map Sketch

Lat. Long.

Party Member	Status	Injuries	Treatment

Date ____________

Conditions

Weather

Terrain

Food Inventory

Rations ☐

Water ☐

Hunting ☐

Fishing ☐

Foraging ☐

Journey

Distance Covered

Trail Markers Used

Landmarks Sighted

Animal Prints

Shelter

Shelter Constructed ☐

Type of Shelter

Clothing/Coverings ☐

Waterproof ☐

Animal proof ☐

Sunproof ☐

Fire Started ☐

Map Sketch

Lat.

Long.

Party Member	Status	Injuries	Treatment

Date

Conditions

Weather

Terrain

Shelter

Shelter Constructed ☐

Type of Shelter

Clothing/Coverings ☐

Waterproof ☐

Animal proof ☐

Sunproof ☐

Fire Started ☐

Food Inventory

Rations ☐

Water ☐

Hunting ☐

Fishing ☐

Foraging ☐

Journey

Distance Covered

Trail Markers Used

Landmarks Sighted

Animal Prints

Map Sketch

Lat. Long.

Party Member	Status	Injuries	Treatment

Date

Conditions

Weather

Terrain

Shelter

Shelter Constructed ☐

Type of Shelter

Clothing/Coverings ☐

Waterproof ☐

Animal proof ☐

Sunproof ☐

Fire Started ☐

Food Inventory

Rations ☐

Water ☐

Hunting ☐

Fishing ☐

Foraging ☐

Journey

Distance Covered

Trail Markers Used

Landmarks Sighted

Animal Prints

Map Sketch

Lat. Long.

Party Member	Status	Injuries	Treatment

Date

Conditions

Weather

Terrain

Shelter

Shelter Constructed ☐

Type of Shelter

Clothing/Coverings ☐

Waterproof ☐

Animal proof ☐

Sunproof ☐

Fire Started ☐

Food Inventory

Rations ☐

Water ☐

Hunting ☐

Fishing ☐

Foraging ☐

Journey

Distance Covered

Trail Markers Used

Landmarks Sighted

Animal Prints

Map Sketch

Lat. Long.

Party Member	Status	Injuries	Treatment

Date

Conditions

Weather

Terrain

Shelter

Shelter Constructed ☐

Type of Shelter

Clothing/Coverings ☐

Waterproof ☐

Animal proof ☐

Sunproof ☐

Fire Started ☐

Food Inventory

Rations ☐

Water ☐

Hunting ☐

Fishing ☐

Foraging ☐

Journey

Distance Covered

Trail Markers Used

Landmarks Sighted

Animal Prints

Map Sketch

Lat. Long.

Party Member	Status	Injuries	Treatment

Date ____________

Conditions

Weather

Terrain

Food Inventory

Rations ☐

Water ☐

Hunting ☐

Fishing ☐

Foraging ☐

Journey

Distance Covered

Trail Markers Used

Landmarks Sighted

Animal Prints

Shelter

Shelter Constructed ☐

Type of Shelter

Clothing/Coverings ☐

Waterproof ☐

Animal proof ☐

Sunproof ☐

Fire Started ☐

Map Sketch

Lat. Long.

Party Member	Status	Injuries	Treatment

Date

Conditions

Weather

Terrain

Shelter

Shelter Constructed ☐

Type of Shelter

Clothing/Coverings ☐

Waterproof ☐

Animal proof ☐

Sunproof ☐

Fire Started ☐

Food Inventory

Rations ☐

Water ☐

Hunting ☐

Fishing ☐

Foraging ☐

Journey

Distance Covered

Trail Markers Used

Landmarks Sighted

Animal Prints

Map Sketch

Lat. Long.

Party Member	Status	Injuries	Treatment

Date

Conditions

Weather

Terrain

Shelter

Shelter Constructed ☐

Type of Shelter

Clothing/Coverings ☐

Waterproof ☐

Animal proof ☐

Sunproof ☐

Fire Started ☐

Food Inventory

Rations ☐

Water ☐

Hunting ☐

Fishing ☐

Foraging ☐

Journey

Distance Covered

Trail Markers Used

Landmarks Sighted

Animal Prints

Map Sketch

Lat. Long.

Party Member	Status	Injuries	Treatment

Date

Conditions

Weather

Terrain

Food Inventory

Rations ☐

Water ☐

Hunting ☐

Fishing ☐

Foraging ☐

Journey

Distance Covered

Trail Markers Used

Landmarks Sighted

Animal Prints

Shelter

Shelter Constructed ☐

Type of Shelter

Clothing/Coverings ☐

Waterproof ☐

Animal proof ☐

Sunproof ☐

Fire Started ☐

Map Sketch

Lat. Long.

Party Member	Status	Injuries	Treatment

Date

Conditions

Weather

Terrain

Shelter

Shelter Constructed ☐

Type of Shelter

Clothing/Coverings ☐

Waterproof ☐

Animal proof ☐

Sunproof ☐

Fire Started ☐

Food Inventory

Rations ☐

Water ☐

Hunting ☐

Fishing ☐

Foraging ☐

Journey

Distance Covered

Trail Markers Used

Landmarks Sighted

Animal Prints

Map Sketch

Lat. Long.

Party Member	Status	Injuries	Treatment

Date

Conditions

Weather

Terrain

Shelter

Shelter Constructed ☐

Type of Shelter

Clothing/Coverings ☐

Waterproof ☐

Animal proof ☐

Sunproof ☐

Fire Started ☐

Food Inventory

Rations ☐

Water ☐

Hunting ☐

Fishing ☐

Foraging ☐

Journey

Distance Covered

Trail Markers Used

Landmarks Sighted

Animal Prints

Map Sketch

Lat. Long.

Party Member	Status	Injuries	Treatment

Date

Conditions

Weather

Terrain

Shelter

Shelter Constructed ☐

Type of Shelter

Clothing/Coverings ☐

Waterproof ☐

Animal proof ☐

Sunproof ☐

Fire Started ☐

Food Inventory

Rations ☐

Water ☐

Hunting ☐

Fishing ☐

Foraging ☐

Journey

Distance Covered

Trail Markers Used

Landmarks Sighted

Animal Prints

Map Sketch

Lat. Long.

Party Member	Status	Injuries	Treatment

Date

Conditions

Weather

Terrain

Shelter

Shelter Constructed ☐

Type of Shelter

Clothing/Coverings ☐

Waterproof ☐

Animal proof ☐

Sunproof ☐

Fire Started ☐

Food Inventory

Rations ☐

Water ☐

Hunting ☐

Fishing ☐

Foraging ☐

Journey

Distance Covered

Trail Markers Used

Landmarks Sighted

Animal Prints

Map Sketch

Lat. Long.

Party Member	Status	Injuries	Treatment

Date

Conditions

Weather

Terrain

Shelter

Shelter Constructed ☐

Type of Shelter

Clothing/Coverings ☐

Waterproof ☐

Animal proof ☐

Sunproof ☐

Fire Started ☐

Food Inventory

Rations ☐

Water ☐

Hunting ☐

Fishing ☐

Foraging ☐

Journey

Distance Covered

Trail Markers Used

Landmarks Sighted

Animal Prints

Map Sketch

Lat. Long.

Party Member	Status	Injuries	Treatment

Date

Conditions

Weather

Terrain

Shelter

Shelter Constructed ☐

Type of Shelter

Clothing/Coverings ☐

Waterproof ☐

Animal proof ☐

Sunproof ☐

Fire Started ☐

Food Inventory

Rations ☐

Water ☐

Hunting ☐

Fishing ☐

Foraging ☐

Journey

Distance Covered

Trail Markers Used

Landmarks Sighted

Animal Prints

Map Sketch

Lat. Long.

Party Member	Status	Injuries	Treatment

Date

Conditions

Weather

Terrain

Shelter

Shelter Constructed ☐

Type of Shelter

Clothing/Coverings ☐

Waterproof ☐

Animal proof ☐

Sunproof ☐

Fire Started ☐

Food Inventory

Rations ☐

Water ☐

Hunting ☐

Fishing ☐

Foraging ☐

Journey

Distance Covered

Trail Markers Used

Landmarks Sighted

Animal Prints

Map Sketch

Lat. Long.

Party Member	Status	Injuries	Treatment

Date ____________

Conditions

Weather

Terrain

Food Inventory

Rations ☐

Water ☐

Hunting ☐

Fishing ☐

Foraging ☐

Journey

Distance Covered

Trail Markers Used

Landmarks Sighted

Animal Prints

Shelter

Shelter Constructed ☐

Type of Shelter

Clothing/Coverings ☐

Waterproof ☐

Animal proof ☐

Sunproof ☐

Fire Started ☐

Map Sketch

Lat. Long.

Party Member	Status	Injuries	Treatment

Date ____________

Conditions

Weather

Terrain

Shelter

Shelter Constructed ☐

Type of Shelter

Clothing/Coverings ☐

Waterproof ☐

Animal proof ☐

Sunproof ☐

Fire Started ☐

Food Inventory

Rations ☐

Water ☐

Hunting ☐

Fishing ☐

Foraging ☐

Journey

Distance Covered

Trail Markers Used

Landmarks Sighted

Animal Prints

Map Sketch

Lat. Long.

Party Member	Status	Injuries	Treatment

Date

Conditions

Weather

Terrain

Shelter

Shelter Constructed ☐

Type of Shelter

Clothing/Coverings ☐

Waterproof ☐

Animal proof ☐

Sunproof ☐

Fire Started ☐

Food Inventory

Rations ☐

Water ☐

Hunting ☐

Fishing ☐

Foraging ☐

Journey

Distance Covered

Trail Markers Used

Landmarks Sighted

Animal Prints

Map Sketch

Lat. Long.

Party Member	Status	Injuries	Treatment

Date ____________

Conditions

Weather

Terrain

Shelter

Shelter Constructed ☐

Type of Shelter

Clothing/Coverings ☐

Waterproof ☐

Animal proof ☐

Sunproof ☐

Fire Started ☐

Food Inventory

Rations ☐

Water ☐

Hunting ☐

Fishing ☐

Foraging ☐

Journey

Distance Covered

Trail Markers Used

Landmarks Sighted

Animal Prints

Map Sketch

Lat. Long.

Party Member	Status	Injuries	Treatment

Date

Conditions

Weather

Terrain

Shelter

Shelter Constructed ☐

Type of Shelter

Clothing/Coverings ☐

Waterproof ☐

Animal proof ☐

Sunproof ☐

Fire Started ☐

Food Inventory

Rations ☐

Water ☐

Hunting ☐

Fishing ☐

Foraging ☐

Journey

Distance Covered

Trail Markers Used

Landmarks Sighted

Animal Prints

Map Sketch

Lat. Long.

Party Member	Status	Injuries	Treatment

Date

Conditions

Weather

Terrain

Shelter

Shelter Constructed ☐

Type of Shelter

Clothing/Coverings ☐

Waterproof ☐

Animal proof ☐

Sunproof ☐

Fire Started ☐

Food Inventory

Rations ☐

Water ☐

Hunting ☐

Fishing ☐

Foraging ☐

Journey

Distance Covered

Trail Markers Used

Landmarks Sighted

Animal Prints

Map Sketch

Lat. Long.

Party Member	Status	Injuries	Treatment

Date

Conditions

Weather

Terrain

Shelter

Shelter Constructed ☐

Type of Shelter

Clothing/Coverings ☐

Waterproof ☐

Animal proof ☐

Sunproof ☐

Fire Started ☐

Food Inventory

Rations ☐

Water ☐

Hunting ☐

Fishing ☐

Foraging ☐

Journey

Distance Covered

Trail Markers Used

Landmarks Sighted

Animal Prints

Map Sketch

Lat. Long.

Party Member	Status	Injuries	Treatment

Date

Conditions

Weather

Terrain

Shelter

Shelter Constructed ☐

Type of Shelter

Clothing/Coverings ☐

Waterproof ☐

Animal proof ☐

Sunproof ☐

Fire Started ☐

Food Inventory

Rations ☐

Water ☐

Hunting ☐

Fishing ☐

Foraging ☐

Journey

Distance Covered

Trail Markers Used

Landmarks Sighted

Animal Prints

Map Sketch

Lat.

Long.

Party Member	Status	Injuries	Treatment

Date

Conditions

Weather

Terrain

Food Inventory

Rations ☐

Water ☐

Hunting ☐

Fishing ☐

Foraging ☐

Journey

Distance Covered

Trail Markers Used

Landmarks Sighted

Animal Prints

Shelter

Shelter Constructed ☐

Type of Shelter

Clothing/Coverings ☐

Waterproof ☐

Animal proof ☐

Sunproof ☐

Fire Started ☐

Map Sketch

Lat. Long.

Party Member	Status	Injuries	Treatment

Date ____________

Conditions

Weather

Terrain

Shelter

Shelter Constructed ☐

Type of Shelter

Clothing/Coverings ☐

Waterproof ☐

Animal proof ☐

Sunproof ☐

Fire Started ☐

Food Inventory

Rations ☐

Water ☐

Hunting ☐

Fishing ☐

Foraging ☐

Journey

Distance Covered

Trail Markers Used

Landmarks Sighted

Animal Prints

Map Sketch

Lat. Long.

Party Member	Status	Injuries	Treatment

Date ______

Conditions

Weather

Terrain

Shelter

Shelter Constructed ☐

Type of Shelter

Clothing/Coverings ☐

Waterproof ☐

Animal proof ☐

Sunproof ☐

Fire Started ☐

Food Inventory

Rations ☐

Water ☐

Hunting ☐

Fishing ☐

Foraging ☐

Journey

Distance Covered

Trail Markers Used

Landmarks Sighted

Animal Prints

Map Sketch

Lat. Long.

Party Member	Status	Injuries	Treatment

Date

Conditions

Weather

Terrain

Shelter

Shelter Constructed ☐

Type of Shelter

Clothing/Coverings ☐

Waterproof ☐

Animal proof ☐

Sunproof ☐

Fire Started ☐

Food Inventory

Rations ☐

Water ☐

Hunting ☐

Fishing ☐

Foraging ☐

Journey

Distance Covered

Trail Markers Used

Landmarks Sighted

Animal Prints

Map Sketch

Lat. Long.

Party Member	Status	Injuries	Treatment

Date

Conditions

Weather

Terrain

Shelter

Shelter Constructed ☐

Type of Shelter

Clothing/Coverings ☐

Waterproof ☐

Animal proof ☐

Sunproof ☐

Fire Started ☐

Food Inventory

Rations ☐

Water ☐

Hunting ☐

Fishing ☐

Foraging ☐

Journey

Distance Covered

Trail Markers Used

Landmarks Sighted

Animal Prints

Map Sketch

Lat. Long.

Party Member	Status	Injuries	Treatment

Date

Conditions

Weather

Terrain

Shelter

Shelter Constructed ☐

Type of Shelter

Clothing/Coverings ☐

Waterproof ☐

Animal proof ☐

Sunproof ☐

Fire Started ☐

Food Inventory

Rations ☐

Water ☐

Hunting ☐

Fishing ☐

Foraging ☐

Journey

Distance Covered

Trail Markers Used

Landmarks Sighted

Animal Prints

Map Sketch

Lat. Long.

Party Member	Status	Injuries	Treatment

Date ____________

Conditions

Weather

Terrain

Shelter

Shelter Constructed ☐

Type of Shelter

Clothing/Coverings ☐

Waterproof ☐

Animal proof ☐

Sunproof ☐

Fire Started ☐

Food Inventory

Rations ☐

Water ☐

Hunting ☐

Fishing ☐

Foraging ☐

Journey

Distance Covered

Trail Markers Used

Landmarks Sighted

Animal Prints

Map Sketch

Lat.

Long.

Party Member	Status	Injuries	Treatment

Date

Conditions

Weather

Terrain

Food Inventory

Rations ☐

Water ☐

Hunting ☐

Fishing ☐

Foraging ☐

Journey

Distance Covered

Trail Markers Used

Landmarks Sighted

Animal Prints

Shelter

Shelter Constructed ☐

Type of Shelter

Clothing/Coverings ☐

Waterproof ☐

Animal proof ☐

Sunproof ☐

Fire Started ☐

Map Sketch

Lat. Long.

Party Member	Status	Injuries	Treatment

Date

Conditions

Weather

Terrain

Food Inventory

Rations ☐

Water ☐

Hunting ☐

Fishing ☐

Foraging ☐

Journey

Distance Covered

Trail Markers Used

Landmarks Sighted

Animal Prints

Shelter

Shelter Constructed ☐

Type of Shelter

Clothing/Coverings ☐

Waterproof ☐

Animal proof ☐

Sunproof ☐

Fire Started ☐

Map Sketch

Lat. Long.

Party Member	Status	Injuries	Treatment

Date ______________

Conditions

Weather

Terrain

Shelter

Shelter Constructed ☐

Type of Shelter

____

____

____

Clothing/Coverings ☐

Waterproof ☐

Animal proof ☐

Sunproof ☐

Fire Started ☐

Food Inventory

Rations ☐

____

____

____

____

Water ☐

Hunting ☐

____

____

____

Fishing ☐

____

____

____

Foraging ☐

____

____

____

Journey

Distance Covered

Trail Markers Used

Landmarks Sighted

Animal Prints

Map Sketch

Lat.

Long.

Party Member	Status	Injuries	Treatment

Date

Conditions

Weather

Terrain

Food Inventory

Rations ☐

Water ☐

Hunting ☐

Fishing ☐

Foraging ☐

Journey

Distance Covered

Trail Markers Used

Landmarks Sighted

Animal Prints

Shelter

Shelter Constructed ☐

Type of Shelter

Clothing/Coverings ☐

Waterproof ☐

Animal proof ☐

Sunproof ☐

Fire Started ☐

Map Sketch

Lat. Long.

Party Member	Status	Injuries	Treatment

Date ____________

Conditions

Weather

Terrain

Shelter

Shelter Constructed ☐

Type of Shelter

Clothing/Coverings ☐

Waterproof ☐

Animal proof ☐

Sunproof ☐

Fire Started ☐

Food Inventory

Rations ☐

Water ☐

Hunting ☐

Fishing ☐

Foraging ☐

Journey

Distance Covered

Trail Markers Used

Landmarks Sighted

Animal Prints

Map Sketch

Lat. Long.

Party Member	Status	Injuries	Treatment

Date ____________

Conditions

Weather

Terrain

Food Inventory

Rations ☐

Water ☐

Hunting ☐

Fishing ☐

Foraging ☐

Journey

Distance Covered

Trail Markers Used

Landmarks Sighted

Animal Prints

Shelter

Shelter Constructed ☐

Type of Shelter

Clothing/Coverings ☐

Waterproof ☐

Animal proof ☐

Sunproof ☐

Fire Started ☐

Map Sketch

Lat.

Long.

Party Member	Status	Injuries	Treatment

Date

Conditions

Weather

Terrain

Shelter

Shelter Constructed ☐

Type of Shelter

Clothing/Coverings ☐

Waterproof ☐

Animal proof ☐

Sunproof ☐

Fire Started ☐

Food Inventory

Rations ☐

Water ☐

Hunting ☐

Fishing ☐

Foraging ☐

Journey

Distance Covered

Trail Markers Used

Landmarks Sighted

Animal Prints

Map Sketch

Lat. Long.

Party Member	Status	Injuries	Treatment

Date ____________

Conditions

Weather

Terrain

Shelter

Shelter Constructed ☐

Type of Shelter

Clothing/Coverings ☐

Waterproof ☐

Animal proof ☐

Sunproof ☐

Fire Started ☐

Food Inventory

Rations ☐

Water ☐

Hunting ☐

Fishing ☐

Foraging ☐

Journey

Distance Covered

Trail Markers Used

Landmarks Sighted

Animal Prints

Map Sketch

Lat.

Long.

Party Member	Status	Injuries	Treatment

Date

Conditions

Weather

Terrain

Shelter

Shelter Constructed ☐

Type of Shelter

Clothing/Coverings ☐

Waterproof ☐

Animal proof ☐

Sunproof ☐

Fire Started ☐

Food Inventory

Rations ☐

Water ☐

Hunting ☐

Fishing ☐

Foraging ☐

Journey

Distance Covered

Trail Markers Used

Landmarks Sighted

Animal Prints

Map Sketch

Lat. Long.

Party Member	Status	Injuries	Treatment

Date

Conditions

Weather

Terrain

Shelter

Shelter Constructed ☐

Type of Shelter

Clothing/Coverings ☐

Waterproof ☐

Animal proof ☐

Sunproof ☐

Fire Started ☐

Food Inventory

Rations ☐

Water ☐

Hunting ☐

Fishing ☐

Foraging ☐

Journey

Distance Covered

Trail Markers Used

Landmarks Sighted

Animal Prints

Map Sketch

Lat. Long.

Party Member	Status	Injuries	Treatment

Date ____________

Conditions

Weather

Terrain

Shelter

Shelter Constructed ☐

Type of Shelter

Clothing/Coverings ☐

Waterproof ☐

Animal proof ☐

Sunproof ☐

Fire Started ☐

Food Inventory

Rations ☐

Water ☐

Hunting ☐

Fishing ☐

Foraging ☐

Journey

Distance Covered

Trail Markers Used

Landmarks Sighted

Animal Prints

Map Sketch

Lat.

Long.

Party Member	Status	Injuries	Treatment

Date ______________

Conditions

Weather

Terrain

Shelter

Shelter Constructed ☐

Type of Shelter

Clothing/Coverings ☐

Waterproof ☐

Animal proof ☐

Sunproof ☐

Fire Started ☐

Food Inventory

Rations ☐

Water ☐

Hunting ☐

Fishing ☐

Foraging ☐

Journey

Distance Covered

Trail Markers Used

Landmarks Sighted

Animal Prints

Map Sketch

Lat. Long.

Party Member	Status	Injuries	Treatment

Date

Conditions

Weather

Terrain

Shelter

Shelter Constructed ☐

Type of Shelter

Clothing/Coverings ☐

Waterproof ☐

Animal proof ☐

Sunproof ☐

Fire Started ☐

Food Inventory

Rations ☐

Water ☐

Hunting ☐

Fishing ☐

Foraging ☐

Journey

Distance Covered

Trail Markers Used

Landmarks Sighted

Animal Prints

Map Sketch

Lat. Long.

Party Member	Status	Injuries	Treatment

Date ____________

Conditions

Weather

Terrain

Shelter

Shelter Constructed ☐

Type of Shelter

Clothing/Coverings ☐

Waterproof ☐

Animal proof ☐

Sunproof ☐

Fire Started ☐

Food Inventory

Rations ☐

Water ☐

Hunting ☐

Fishing ☐

Foraging ☐

Journey

Distance Covered

Trail Markers Used

Landmarks Sighted

Animal Prints

Map Sketch

Lat. Long.

Party Member	Status	Injuries	Treatment

Date

Conditions

Weather

Terrain

Shelter

Shelter Constructed ☐

Type of Shelter

Clothing/Coverings ☐

Waterproof ☐

Animal proof ☐

Sunproof ☐

Fire Started ☐

Food Inventory

Rations ☐

Water ☐

Hunting ☐

Fishing ☐

Foraging ☐

Journey

Distance Covered

Trail Markers Used

Landmarks Sighted

Animal Prints

Map Sketch

Lat. Long.

Party Member	Status	Injuries	Treatment

Date ____________

Conditions

Weather

Terrain

Shelter

Shelter Constructed ☐

Type of Shelter

Clothing/Coverings ☐

Waterproof ☐

Animal proof ☐

Sunproof ☐

Fire Started ☐

Food Inventory

Rations ☐

Water ☐

Hunting ☐

Fishing ☐

Foraging ☐

Journey

Distance Covered

Trail Markers Used

Landmarks Sighted

Animal Prints

Map Sketch

Lat. Long.

Party Member	Status	Injuries	Treatment

Date ______________

Conditions

Weather

Terrain

Shelter

Shelter Constructed ☐

Type of Shelter

____

____

____

Clothing/Coverings ☐

Waterproof ☐

Animal proof ☐

Sunproof ☐

Fire Started ☐

Food Inventory

Rations ☐

____

____

____

____

Water ☐

Hunting ☐

____

____

____

Fishing ☐

____

____

____

Foraging ☐

____

____

____

Journey

Distance Covered

Trail Markers Used

Landmarks Sighted

Animal Prints

Map Sketch

Lat.

Long.

Party Member	Status	Injuries	Treatment

Date ______________

Conditions

Weather

Terrain

Food Inventory

Rations ☐

Water ☐

Hunting ☐

Fishing ☐

Foraging ☐

Journey

Distance Covered

Trail Markers Used

Landmarks Sighted

Animal Prints

Shelter

Shelter Constructed ☐

Type of Shelter

Clothing/Coverings ☐

Waterproof ☐

Animal proof ☐

Sunproof ☐

Fire Started ☐

Map Sketch

Lat.

Long.

Party Member	Status	Injuries	Treatment

Date

Conditions

Weather

Terrain

Food Inventory

Rations ☐

Water ☐

Hunting ☐

Fishing ☐

Foraging ☐

Journey

Distance Covered

Trail Markers Used

Landmarks Sighted

Animal Prints

Shelter

Shelter Constructed ☐

Type of Shelter

Clothing/Coverings ☐

Waterproof ☐

Animal proof ☐

Sunproof ☐

Fire Started ☐

Map Sketch

Lat. Long.

Party Member	Status	Injuries	Treatment

Date ______________

Conditions

Weather

Terrain

Shelter

Shelter Constructed ☐

Type of Shelter

Clothing/Coverings ☐

Waterproof ☐

Animal proof ☐

Sunproof ☐

Fire Started ☐

Food Inventory

Rations ☐

Water ☐

Hunting ☐

Fishing ☐

Foraging ☐

Journey

Distance Covered

Trail Markers Used

Landmarks Sighted

Animal Prints

Map Sketch

Lat. Long.

Party Member	Status	Injuries	Treatment

Date

Conditions

Weather

Terrain

Shelter

Shelter Constructed ☐

Type of Shelter

Clothing/Coverings ☐

Waterproof ☐

Animal proof ☐

Sunproof ☐

Fire Started ☐

Food Inventory

Rations ☐

Water ☐

Hunting ☐

Fishing ☐

Foraging ☐

Journey

Distance Covered

Trail Markers Used

Landmarks Sighted

Animal Prints

Map Sketch

Lat. Long.

Party Member	Status	Injuries	Treatment

Date

Conditions

Weather

Terrain

Shelter

Shelter Constructed ☐

Type of Shelter

Clothing/Coverings ☐

Waterproof ☐

Animal proof ☐

Sunproof ☐

Fire Started ☐

Food Inventory

Rations ☐

Water ☐

Hunting ☐

Fishing ☐

Foraging ☐

Journey

Distance Covered

Trail Markers Used

Landmarks Sighted

Animal Prints

Map Sketch

Lat.

Long.

Party Member	Status	Injuries	Treatment

Date

Conditions

Weather

Terrain

Shelter

Shelter Constructed ☐

Type of Shelter

Clothing/Coverings ☐

Waterproof ☐

Animal proof ☐

Sunproof ☐

Fire Started ☐

Food Inventory

Rations ☐

Water ☐

Hunting ☐

Fishing ☐

Foraging ☐

Journey

Distance Covered

Trail Markers Used

Landmarks Sighted

Animal Prints

Map Sketch

Lat. Long.

Party Member	Status	Injuries	Treatment

Date

Conditions

Weather

Terrain

Food Inventory

Rations ☐

Water ☐

Hunting ☐

Fishing ☐

Foraging ☐

Journey

Distance Covered

Trail Markers Used

Landmarks Sighted

Animal Prints

Shelter

Shelter Constructed ☐

Type of Shelter

Clothing/Coverings ☐

Waterproof ☐

Animal proof ☐

Sunproof ☐

Fire Started ☐

Map Sketch

Lat.

Long.

Party Member	Status	Injuries	Treatment

Date ______________

Conditions

Weather

Terrain

Shelter

Shelter Constructed ☐

Type of Shelter

Clothing/Coverings ☐

Waterproof ☐

Animal proof ☐

Sunproof ☐

Fire Started ☐

Food Inventory

Rations ☐

Water ☐

Hunting ☐

Fishing ☐

Foraging ☐

Journey

Distance Covered

Trail Markers Used

Landmarks Sighted

Animal Prints

Map Sketch

Lat. Long.

Party Member	Status	Injuries	Treatment

Date ______

Conditions

Weather

Terrain

Food Inventory

Rations ☐

Water ☐

Hunting ☐

Fishing ☐

Foraging ☐

Journey

Distance Covered

Trail Markers Used

Landmarks Sighted

Animal Prints

Shelter

Shelter Constructed ☐

Type of Shelter

Clothing/Coverings ☐

Waterproof ☐

Animal proof ☐

Sunproof ☐

Fire Started ☐

Map Sketch

Lat. Long.

Party Member	Status	Injuries	Treatment

Date ____________

Conditions

Weather

Terrain

Shelter

Shelter Constructed ☐

Type of Shelter

Clothing/Coverings ☐

Waterproof ☐

Animal proof ☐

Sunproof ☐

Fire Started ☐

Food Inventory

Rations ☐

Water ☐

Hunting ☐

Fishing ☐

Foraging ☐

Journey

Distance Covered

Trail Markers Used

Landmarks Sighted

Animal Prints

Map Sketch

Lat. Long.

Party Member	Status	Injuries	Treatment

Date

Conditions

Weather

Terrain

Shelter

Shelter Constructed ☐

Type of Shelter

Clothing/Coverings ☐

Waterproof ☐

Animal proof ☐

Sunproof ☐

Fire Started ☐

Food Inventory

Rations ☐

Water ☐

Hunting ☐

Fishing ☐

Foraging ☐

Journey

Distance Covered

Trail Markers Used

Landmarks Sighted

Animal Prints

Map Sketch

Lat.

Long.

Party Member	Status	Injuries	Treatment

Date ______________

Conditions

Weather

Terrain

Shelter

Shelter Constructed ☐

Type of Shelter

Clothing/Coverings ☐

Waterproof ☐

Animal proof ☐

Sunproof ☐

Fire Started ☐

Food Inventory

Rations ☐

Water ☐

Hunting ☐

Fishing ☐

Foraging ☐

Journey

Distance Covered

Trail Markers Used

Landmarks Sighted

Animal Prints

Map Sketch

Lat. Long.

Party Member	Status	Injuries	Treatment

Date

Conditions

Weather

Terrain

Food Inventory

Rations ☐

Water ☐

Hunting ☐

Fishing ☐

Foraging ☐

Journey

Distance Covered

Trail Markers Used

Landmarks Sighted

Animal Prints

Shelter

Shelter Constructed ☐

Type of Shelter

Clothing/Coverings ☐

Waterproof ☐

Animal proof ☐

Sunproof ☐

Fire Started ☐

Map Sketch

Lat.

Long.

Party Member	Status	Injuries	Treatment

Date

Conditions

Weather

Terrain

Shelter

Shelter Constructed ☐

Type of Shelter

Clothing/Coverings ☐

Waterproof ☐

Animal proof ☐

Sunproof ☐

Fire Started ☐

Food Inventory

Rations ☐

Water ☐

Hunting ☐

Fishing ☐

Foraging ☐

Journey

Distance Covered

Trail Markers Used

Landmarks Sighted

Animal Prints

Map Sketch

Lat. Long.

Party Member	Status	Injuries	Treatment

Date ______________

Conditions

Weather

Terrain

Shelter

Shelter Constructed ☐

Type of Shelter

Clothing/Coverings ☐

Waterproof ☐

Animal proof ☐

Sunproof ☐

Fire Started ☐

Food Inventory

Rations ☐

Water ☐

Hunting ☐

Fishing ☐

Foraging ☐

Journey

Distance Covered

Trail Markers Used

Landmarks Sighted

Animal Prints

Map Sketch

Lat.

Long.

Party Member	Status	Injuries	Treatment

Date

Conditions

Weather

Terrain

Shelter

Shelter Constructed ☐

Type of Shelter

Clothing/Coverings ☐

Waterproof ☐

Animal proof ☐

Sunproof ☐

Fire Started ☐

Food Inventory

Rations ☐

Water ☐

Hunting ☐

Fishing ☐

Foraging ☐

Journey

Distance Covered

Trail Markers Used

Landmarks Sighted

Animal Prints

Map Sketch

Lat. Long.

Party Member	Status	Injuries	Treatment

Date

Conditions

Weather

Terrain

Shelter

Shelter Constructed ☐

Type of Shelter

Clothing/Coverings ☐

Waterproof ☐

Animal proof ☐

Sunproof ☐

Fire Started ☐

Food Inventory

Rations ☐

Water ☐

Hunting ☐

Fishing ☐

Foraging ☐

Journey

Distance Covered

Trail Markers Used

Landmarks Sighted

Animal Prints

Map Sketch

Lat.

Long.

Party Member	Status	Injuries	Treatment

Date ____________

Conditions

Weather

Terrain

Shelter

Shelter Constructed ☐

Type of Shelter

Clothing/Coverings ☐

Waterproof ☐

Animal proof ☐

Sunproof ☐

Fire Started ☐

Food Inventory

Rations ☐

Water ☐

Hunting ☐

Fishing ☐

Foraging ☐

Journey

Distance Covered

Trail Markers Used

Landmarks Sighted

Animal Prints

Map Sketch

Lat.

Long.

Party Member	Status	Injuries	Treatment

Date ______________

Conditions

Weather

Terrain

Shelter

Shelter Constructed ☐

Type of Shelter

____

____

____

Clothing/Coverings ☐

Waterproof ☐

Animal proof ☐

Sunproof ☐

Fire Started ☐

Food Inventory

Rations ☐

____

____

____

____

Water ☐

Hunting ☐

____

____

____

Fishing ☐

____

____

____

Foraging ☐

____

____

____

Journey

Distance Covered

Trail Markers Used

Landmarks Sighted

Animal Prints

Map Sketch

Lat. Long.

Party Member	Status	Injuries	Treatment

Date

Conditions

Weather

Terrain

Shelter

Shelter Constructed ☐

Type of Shelter

Clothing/Coverings ☐

Waterproof ☐

Animal proof ☐

Sunproof ☐

Fire Started ☐

Food Inventory

Rations ☐

Water ☐

Hunting ☐

Fishing ☐

Foraging ☐

Journey

Distance Covered

Trail Markers Used

Landmarks Sighted

Animal Prints

Map Sketch

Lat. Long.

Party Member	Status	Injuries	Treatment

Date ____________

Conditions

Weather

Terrain

Shelter

Shelter Constructed ☐

Type of Shelter

Clothing/Coverings ☐

Waterproof ☐

Animal proof ☐

Sunproof ☐

Fire Started ☐

Food Inventory

Rations ☐

Water ☐

Hunting ☐

Fishing ☐

Foraging ☐

Journey

Distance Covered

Trail Markers Used

Landmarks Sighted

Animal Prints

Map Sketch

Lat. Long.

Party Member	Status	Injuries	Treatment

Date ____________

Conditions

Weather

Terrain

Food Inventory

Rations ☐

Water ☐

Hunting ☐

Fishing ☐

Foraging ☐

Journey

Distance Covered

Trail Markers Used

Landmarks Sighted

Animal Prints

Shelter

Shelter Constructed ☐

Type of Shelter

Clothing/Coverings ☐

Waterproof ☐

Animal proof ☐

Sunproof ☐

Fire Started ☐

Map Sketch

Lat. Long.

Party Member	Status	Injuries	Treatment

Date ______________________

Conditions

Weather

Terrain

Shelter

Shelter Constructed ☐

Type of Shelter

____

____

____

Clothing/Coverings ☐

Waterproof ☐

Animal proof ☐

Sunproof ☐

Fire Started ☐

Food Inventory

Rations ☐

____

____

____

____

Water ☐

Hunting ☐

____

____

____

Fishing ☐

____

____

____

Foraging ☐

____

____

____

Journey

Distance Covered

Trail Markers Used

Landmarks Sighted

Animal Prints

Map Sketch

Lat. Long.

Party Member	Status	Injuries	Treatment

Date

Conditions

Weather

Terrain

Shelter

Shelter Constructed ☐

Type of Shelter

Clothing/Coverings ☐

Waterproof ☐

Animal proof ☐

Sunproof ☐

Fire Started ☐

Food Inventory

Rations ☐

Water ☐

Hunting ☐

Fishing ☐

Foraging ☐

Journey

Distance Covered

Trail Markers Used

Landmarks Sighted

Animal Prints

Map Sketch

Lat. Long.

Party Member	Status	Injuries	Treatment

Date

Conditions

Weather

Terrain

Shelter

Shelter Constructed ☐

Type of Shelter

Clothing/Coverings ☐

Waterproof ☐

Animal proof ☐

Sunproof ☐

Fire Started ☐

Food Inventory

Rations ☐

Water ☐

Hunting ☐

Fishing ☐

Foraging ☐

Journey

Distance Covered

Trail Markers Used

Landmarks Sighted

Animal Prints

Map Sketch

Lat.

Long.

Party Member	Status	Injuries	Treatment

Date

Conditions

Weather

Terrain

Shelter

Shelter Constructed ☐

Type of Shelter

Clothing/Coverings ☐

Waterproof ☐

Animal proof ☐

Sunproof ☐

Fire Started ☐

Food Inventory

Rations ☐

Water ☐

Hunting ☐

Fishing ☐

Foraging ☐

Journey

Distance Covered

Trail Markers Used

Landmarks Sighted

Animal Prints

Map Sketch

Lat. Long.

Party Member	Status	Injuries	Treatment

Date

Conditions

Weather

Terrain

Food Inventory

Rations ☐

Water ☐

Hunting ☐

Fishing ☐

Foraging ☐

Journey

Distance Covered

Trail Markers Used

Landmarks Sighted

Animal Prints

Shelter

Shelter Constructed ☐

Type of Shelter

Clothing/Coverings ☐

Waterproof ☐

Animal proof ☐

Sunproof ☐

Fire Started ☐

Map Sketch

Lat. Long.

Party Member	Status	Injuries	Treatment

Date

Conditions

Weather

Terrain

Shelter

Shelter Constructed ☐

Type of Shelter

Clothing/Coverings ☐

Waterproof ☐

Animal proof ☐

Sunproof ☐

Fire Started ☐

Food Inventory

Rations ☐

Water ☐

Hunting ☐

Fishing ☐

Foraging ☐

Journey

Distance Covered

Trail Markers Used

Landmarks Sighted

Animal Prints

Map Sketch

Lat. Long.

Party Member	Status	Injuries	Treatment

Date

Conditions

Weather

Terrain

Shelter

Shelter Constructed ☐

Type of Shelter

Clothing/Coverings ☐

Waterproof ☐

Animal proof ☐

Sunproof ☐

Fire Started ☐

Food Inventory

Rations ☐

Water ☐

Hunting ☐

Fishing ☐

Foraging ☐

Journey

Distance Covered

Trail Markers Used

Landmarks Sighted

Animal Prints

Map Sketch

Lat. Long.

Party Member	Status	Injuries	Treatment

Date ______________

Conditions

Weather

Terrain

Shelter

Shelter Constructed ☐

Type of Shelter

Clothing/Coverings ☐

Waterproof ☐

Animal proof ☐

Sunproof ☐

Fire Started ☐

Food Inventory

Rations ☐

Water ☐

Hunting ☐

Fishing ☐

Foraging ☐

Journey

Distance Covered

Trail Markers Used

Landmarks Sighted

Animal Prints

Map Sketch

Lat.

Long.

Party Member	Status	Injuries	Treatment

Date

Conditions

Weather

Terrain

Shelter

Shelter Constructed ☐

Type of Shelter

Clothing/Coverings ☐

Waterproof ☐

Animal proof ☐

Sunproof ☐

Fire Started ☐

Food Inventory

Rations ☐

Water ☐

Hunting ☐

Fishing ☐

Foraging ☐

Journey

Distance Covered

Trail Markers Used

Landmarks Sighted

Animal Prints

Map Sketch

Lat. Long.

Party Member	Status	Injuries	Treatment

Date

Conditions

Weather

Terrain

Shelter

Shelter Constructed ☐

Type of Shelter

Clothing/Coverings ☐

Waterproof ☐

Animal proof ☐

Sunproof ☐

Fire Started ☐

Food Inventory

Rations ☐

Water ☐

Hunting ☐

Fishing ☐

Foraging ☐

Journey

Distance Covered

Trail Markers Used

Landmarks Sighted

Animal Prints

Map Sketch

Lat. Long.

Party Member	Status	Injuries	Treatment

Date ____________

Conditions

Weather

Terrain

Food Inventory

Rations ☐

Water ☐

Hunting ☐

Fishing ☐

Foraging ☐

Journey

Distance Covered

Trail Markers Used

Landmarks Sighted

Animal Prints

Shelter

Shelter Constructed ☐

Type of Shelter

Clothing/Coverings ☐

Waterproof ☐

Animal proof ☐

Sunproof ☐

Fire Started ☐

Map Sketch

Lat. Long.

Party Member	Status	Injuries	Treatment

Date ________________

Conditions

Weather

Terrain

Food Inventory

Rations ☐

Water ☐

Hunting ☐

Fishing ☐

Foraging ☐

Journey

Distance Covered

Trail Markers Used

Landmarks Sighted

Animal Prints

Shelter

Shelter Constructed ☐

Type of Shelter

Clothing/Coverings ☐

Waterproof ☐

Animal proof ☐

Sunproof ☐

Fire Started ☐

Map Sketch

Lat.

Long.

Party Member	Status	Injuries	Treatment

Date

Conditions

Weather

Terrain

Shelter

Shelter Constructed ☐

Type of Shelter

Clothing/Coverings ☐

Waterproof ☐

Animal proof ☐

Sunproof ☐

Fire Started ☐

Food Inventory

Rations ☐

Water ☐

Hunting ☐

Fishing ☐

Foraging ☐

Journey

Distance Covered

Trail Markers Used

Landmarks Sighted

Animal Prints

Map Sketch

Lat. Long.

Party Member	Status	Injuries	Treatment

Date

Conditions

Weather

Terrain

Shelter

Shelter Constructed ☐

Type of Shelter

Clothing/Coverings ☐

Waterproof ☐

Animal proof ☐

Sunproof ☐

Fire Started ☐

Food Inventory

Rations ☐

Water ☐

Hunting ☐

Fishing ☐

Foraging ☐

Journey

Distance Covered

Trail Markers Used

Landmarks Sighted

Animal Prints

Map Sketch

Lat. Long.

Party Member	Status	Injuries	Treatment

Date

Conditions

Weather

Terrain

Shelter

Shelter Constructed ☐

Type of Shelter

Clothing/Coverings ☐

Waterproof ☐

Animal proof ☐

Sunproof ☐

Fire Started ☐

Food Inventory

Rations ☐

Water ☐

Hunting ☐

Fishing ☐

Foraging ☐

Journey

Distance Covered

Trail Markers Used

Landmarks Sighted

Animal Prints

Map Sketch

Lat. Long.

Party Member	Status	Injuries	Treatment

Date

Conditions

Weather

Terrain

Shelter

Shelter Constructed ☐

Type of Shelter

Clothing/Coverings ☐

Waterproof ☐

Animal proof ☐

Sunproof ☐

Fire Started ☐

Food Inventory

Rations ☐

Water ☐

Hunting ☐

Fishing ☐

Foraging ☐

Journey

Distance Covered

Trail Markers Used

Landmarks Sighted

Animal Prints

Map Sketch

Lat. Long.

Party Member	Status	Injuries	Treatment

Date

Conditions

Weather

Terrain

Shelter

Shelter Constructed ☐

Type of Shelter

Clothing/Coverings ☐

Waterproof ☐

Animal proof ☐

Sunproof ☐

Fire Started ☐

Food Inventory

Rations ☐

Water ☐

Hunting ☐

Fishing ☐

Foraging ☐

Journey

Distance Covered

Trail Markers Used

Landmarks Sighted

Animal Prints

Map Sketch

Lat. Long.

Party Member	Status	Injuries	Treatment

Date

Conditions

Weather

Terrain

Shelter

Shelter Constructed ☐

Type of Shelter

Clothing/Coverings ☐

Waterproof ☐

Animal proof ☐

Sunproof ☐

Fire Started ☐

Food Inventory

Rations ☐

Water ☐

Hunting ☐

Fishing ☐

Foraging ☐

Journey

Distance Covered

Trail Markers Used

Landmarks Sighted

Animal Prints

Map Sketch

Lat. Long.

Party Member	Status	Injuries	Treatment

Date ______

Conditions

Weather

Terrain

Shelter

Shelter Constructed ☐

Type of Shelter

Clothing/Coverings ☐

Waterproof ☐

Animal proof ☐

Sunproof ☐

Fire Started ☐

Food Inventory

Rations ☐

Water ☐

Hunting ☐

Fishing ☐

Foraging ☐

Journey

Distance Covered

Trail Markers Used

Landmarks Sighted

Animal Prints

Map Sketch

Lat. Long.

Party Member	Status	Injuries	Treatment

Date

Conditions

Weather

Terrain

Shelter

Shelter Constructed ☐

Type of Shelter

Clothing/Coverings ☐

Waterproof ☐

Animal proof ☐

Sunproof ☐

Fire Started ☐

Food Inventory

Rations ☐

Water ☐

Hunting ☐

Fishing ☐

Foraging ☐

Journey

Distance Covered

Trail Markers Used

Landmarks Sighted

Animal Prints

Map Sketch

Lat.

Long.

Party Member	Status	Injuries	Treatment

Date

Conditions

Weather

Terrain

Shelter

Shelter Constructed ☐

Type of Shelter

Clothing/Coverings ☐

Waterproof ☐

Animal proof ☐

Sunproof ☐

Fire Started ☐

Food Inventory

Rations ☐

Water ☐

Hunting ☐

Fishing ☐

Foraging ☐

Journey

Distance Covered

Trail Markers Used

Landmarks Sighted

Animal Prints

Map Sketch

Lat. Long.

Party Member	Status	Injuries	Treatment

Date

Conditions

Weather

Terrain

Shelter

Shelter Constructed ☐

Type of Shelter

Clothing/Coverings ☐

Waterproof ☐

Animal proof ☐

Sunproof ☐

Fire Started ☐

Food Inventory

Rations ☐

Water ☐

Hunting ☐

Fishing ☐

Foraging ☐

Journey

Distance Covered

Trail Markers Used

Landmarks Sighted

Animal Prints

Map Sketch

Lat. Long.

Party Member	Status	Injuries	Treatment

Date

Conditions

Weather

Terrain

Shelter

Shelter Constructed ☐

Type of Shelter

Clothing/Coverings ☐

Waterproof ☐

Animal proof ☐

Sunproof ☐

Fire Started ☐

Food Inventory

Rations ☐

Water ☐

Hunting ☐

Fishing ☐

Foraging ☐

Journey

Distance Covered

Trail Markers Used

Landmarks Sighted

Animal Prints

Map Sketch

Lat.

Long.

Party Member	Status	Injuries	Treatment

Date

Conditions

Weather

Terrain

Shelter

Shelter Constructed ☐

Type of Shelter

Clothing/Coverings ☐

Waterproof ☐

Animal proof ☐

Sunproof ☐

Fire Started ☐

Food Inventory

Rations ☐

Water ☐

Hunting ☐

Fishing ☐

Foraging ☐

Journey

Distance Covered

Trail Markers Used

Landmarks Sighted

Animal Prints

Map Sketch

Lat. Long.

Party Member	Status	Injuries	Treatment

Date

Conditions

Weather

Terrain

Shelter

Shelter Constructed ☐

Type of Shelter

Clothing/Coverings ☐

Waterproof ☐

Animal proof ☐

Sunproof ☐

Fire Started ☐

Food Inventory

Rations ☐

Water ☐

Hunting ☐

Fishing ☐

Foraging ☐

Journey

Distance Covered

Trail Markers Used

Landmarks Sighted

Animal Prints

Map Sketch

Lat. Long.

Party Member	Status	Injuries	Treatment

Date

Conditions

Weather

Terrain

Shelter

Shelter Constructed ☐

Type of Shelter

Clothing/Coverings ☐

Waterproof ☐

Animal proof ☐

Sunproof ☐

Fire Started ☐

Food Inventory

Rations ☐

Water ☐

Hunting ☐

Fishing ☐

Foraging ☐

Journey

Distance Covered

Trail Markers Used

Landmarks Sighted

Animal Prints

Map Sketch

Lat.

Long.

Party Member	Status	Injuries	Treatment

Date

Conditions

Weather

Terrain

Shelter

Shelter Constructed ☐

Type of Shelter

Clothing/Coverings ☐

Waterproof ☐

Animal proof ☐

Sunproof ☐

Fire Started ☐

Food Inventory

Rations ☐

Water ☐

Hunting ☐

Fishing ☐

Foraging ☐

Journey

Distance Covered

Trail Markers Used

Landmarks Sighted

Animal Prints

Map Sketch

Lat. Long.

Party Member	Status	Injuries	Treatment

Date

Conditions

Weather

Terrain

Shelter

Shelter Constructed ☐

Type of Shelter

Clothing/Coverings ☐

Waterproof ☐

Animal proof ☐

Sunproof ☐

Fire Started ☐

Food Inventory

Rations ☐

Water ☐

Hunting ☐

Fishing ☐

Foraging ☐

Journey

Distance Covered

Trail Markers Used

Landmarks Sighted

Animal Prints

Map Sketch

Lat.

Long.

Party Member	Status	Injuries	Treatment

Date

Conditions

Weather

Terrain

Shelter

Shelter Constructed ☐

Type of Shelter

Clothing/Coverings ☐

Waterproof ☐

Animal proof ☐

Sunproof ☐

Fire Started ☐

Food Inventory

Rations ☐

Water ☐

Hunting ☐

Fishing ☐

Foraging ☐

Journey

Distance Covered

Trail Markers Used

Landmarks Sighted

Animal Prints

Map Sketch

Lat. Long.

Party Member	Status	Injuries	Treatment

Date ______________

Conditions

Weather

Terrain

Shelter

Shelter Constructed ☐

Type of Shelter

Clothing/Coverings ☐

Waterproof ☐

Animal proof ☐

Sunproof ☐

Fire Started ☐

Food Inventory

Rations ☐

Water ☐

Hunting ☐

Fishing ☐

Foraging ☐

Journey

Distance Covered

Trail Markers Used

Landmarks Sighted

Animal Prints

Map Sketch

Lat. Long.

Party Member	Status	Injuries	Treatment

Date ______________

Conditions

Weather

Terrain

Shelter

Shelter Constructed ☐

Type of Shelter

Clothing/Coverings ☐

Waterproof ☐

Animal proof ☐

Sunproof ☐

Fire Started ☐

Food Inventory

Rations ☐

Water ☐

Hunting ☐

Fishing ☐

Foraging ☐

Journey

Distance Covered

Trail Markers Used

Landmarks Sighted

Animal Prints

Map Sketch

Lat. Long.

Party Member	Status	Injuries	Treatment

Date

Conditions

Weather

Terrain

Shelter

Shelter Constructed ☐

Type of Shelter

Clothing/Coverings ☐

Waterproof ☐

Animal proof ☐

Sunproof ☐

Fire Started ☐

Food Inventory

Rations ☐

Water ☐

Hunting ☐

Fishing ☐

Foraging ☐

Journey

Distance Covered

Trail Markers Used

Landmarks Sighted

Animal Prints

Map Sketch

Lat. Long.

Party Member	Status	Injuries	Treatment

Date

Conditions

Weather

Terrain

Shelter

Shelter Constructed ☐

Type of Shelter

Clothing/Coverings ☐

Waterproof ☐

Animal proof ☐

Sunproof ☐

Fire Started ☐

Food Inventory

Rations ☐

Water ☐

Hunting ☐

Fishing ☐

Foraging ☐

Journey

Distance Covered

Trail Markers Used

Landmarks Sighted

Animal Prints

Map Sketch

Lat. Long.

Party Member	Status	Injuries	Treatment

Date

Conditions

Weather

Terrain

Shelter

Shelter Constructed ☐

Type of Shelter

Clothing/Coverings ☐

Waterproof ☐

Animal proof ☐

Sunproof ☐

Fire Started ☐

Food Inventory

Rations ☐

Water ☐

Hunting ☐

Fishing ☐

Foraging ☐

Journey

Distance Covered

Trail Markers Used

Landmarks Sighted

Animal Prints

Map Sketch

Lat.

Long.

Party Member	Status	Injuries	Treatment

Date

Conditions

Weather

Terrain

Shelter

Shelter Constructed ☐

Type of Shelter

Clothing/Coverings ☐

Waterproof ☐

Animal proof ☐

Sunproof ☐

Fire Started ☐

Food Inventory

Rations ☐

Water ☐

Hunting ☐

Fishing ☐

Foraging ☐

Journey

Distance Covered

Trail Markers Used

Landmarks Sighted

Animal Prints

Map Sketch

Lat.

Long.

Party Member	Status	Injuries	Treatment

Date

Conditions

Weather

Terrain

Shelter

Shelter Constructed ☐

Type of Shelter

Clothing/Coverings ☐

Waterproof ☐

Animal proof ☐

Sunproof ☐

Fire Started ☐

Food Inventory

Rations ☐

Water ☐

Hunting ☐

Fishing ☐

Foraging ☐

Journey

Distance Covered

Trail Markers Used

Landmarks Sighted

Animal Prints

Map Sketch

Lat. Long.

Party Member	Status	Injuries	Treatment

Date

Conditions

Weather

Terrain

Shelter

Shelter Constructed ☐

Type of Shelter

Clothing/Coverings ☐

Waterproof ☐

Animal proof ☐

Sunproof ☐

Fire Started ☐

Food Inventory

Rations ☐

Water ☐

Hunting ☐

Fishing ☐

Foraging ☐

Journey

Distance Covered

Trail Markers Used

Landmarks Sighted

Animal Prints

Map Sketch

Lat. Long.

Party Member	Status	Injuries	Treatment

Date

Conditions

Weather

Terrain

Shelter

Shelter Constructed ☐

Type of Shelter

Clothing/Coverings ☐

Waterproof ☐

Animal proof ☐

Sunproof ☐

Fire Started ☐

Food Inventory

Rations ☐

Water ☐

Hunting ☐

Fishing ☐

Foraging ☐

Journey

Distance Covered

Trail Markers Used

Landmarks Sighted

Animal Prints

Map Sketch

Lat.

Long.

Party Member	Status	Injuries	Treatment

Date

Conditions

Weather

Terrain

Shelter

Shelter Constructed ☐

Type of Shelter

Clothing/Coverings ☐

Waterproof ☐

Animal proof ☐

Sunproof ☐

Fire Started ☐

Food Inventory

Rations ☐

Water ☐

Hunting ☐

Fishing ☐

Foraging ☐

Journey

Distance Covered

Trail Markers Used

Landmarks Sighted

Animal Prints

Map Sketch

Lat.

Long.

Party Member	Status	Injuries	Treatment

Date

Conditions

Weather

Terrain

Shelter

Shelter Constructed ☐

Type of Shelter

Clothing/Coverings ☐

Waterproof ☐

Animal proof ☐

Sunproof ☐

Fire Started ☐

Food Inventory

Rations ☐

Water ☐

Hunting ☐

Fishing ☐

Foraging ☐

Journey

Distance Covered

Trail Markers Used

Landmarks Sighted

Animal Prints

Map Sketch

Lat.

Long.

Party Member	Status	Injuries	Treatment

Date

Conditions

Weather

Terrain

Shelter

Shelter Constructed ☐

Type of Shelter

Clothing/Coverings ☐

Waterproof ☐

Animal proof ☐

Sunproof ☐

Fire Started ☐

Food Inventory

Rations ☐

Water ☐

Hunting ☐

Fishing ☐

Foraging ☐

Journey

Distance Covered

Trail Markers Used

Landmarks Sighted

Animal Prints

Map Sketch

Lat.

Long.

Party Member	Status	Injuries	Treatment

Date

Conditions

Weather

Terrain

Shelter

Shelter Constructed ☐

Type of Shelter

Clothing/Coverings ☐

Waterproof ☐

Animal proof ☐

Sunproof ☐

Fire Started ☐

Food Inventory

Rations ☐

Water ☐

Hunting ☐

Fishing ☐

Foraging ☐

Journey

Distance Covered

Trail Markers Used

Landmarks Sighted

Animal Prints

Map Sketch

Lat. Long.

Party Member	Status	Injuries	Treatment

Date ____________

Conditions

Weather

Terrain

Shelter

Shelter Constructed ☐

Type of Shelter

Clothing/Coverings ☐

Waterproof ☐

Animal proof ☐

Sunproof ☐

Fire Started ☐

Food Inventory

Rations ☐

Water ☐

Hunting ☐

Fishing ☐

Foraging ☐

Journey

Distance Covered

Trail Markers Used

Landmarks Sighted

Animal Prints

Map Sketch

Lat. Long.

Party Member	Status	Injuries	Treatment

Date ______________

Conditions

Weather

Terrain

Food Inventory

Rations ☐

Water ☐

Hunting ☐

Fishing ☐

Foraging ☐

Journey

Distance Covered

Trail Markers Used

Landmarks Sighted

Animal Prints

Shelter

Shelter Constructed ☐

Type of Shelter

Clothing/Coverings ☐

Waterproof ☐

Animal proof ☐

Sunproof ☐

Fire Started ☐

Map Sketch

Lat. Long.

Party Member	Status	Injuries	Treatment

Date

Conditions

Weather

Terrain

Shelter

Shelter Constructed ☐

Type of Shelter

Clothing/Coverings ☐

Waterproof ☐

Animal proof ☐

Sunproof ☐

Fire Started ☐

Food Inventory

Rations ☐

Water ☐

Hunting ☐

Fishing ☐

Foraging ☐

Journey

Distance Covered

Trail Markers Used

Landmarks Sighted

Animal Prints

Map Sketch

Lat.

Long.

Party Member	Status	Injuries	Treatment

Date

Conditions

Weather

Terrain

Shelter

Shelter Constructed ☐

Type of Shelter

Clothing/Coverings ☐

Waterproof ☐

Animal proof ☐

Sunproof ☐

Fire Started ☐

Food Inventory

Rations ☐

Water ☐

Hunting ☐

Fishing ☐

Foraging ☐

Journey

Distance Covered

Trail Markers Used

Landmarks Sighted

Animal Prints

Map Sketch

Lat. Long.

Party Member	Status	Injuries	Treatment

Date

Conditions

Weather

Terrain

Shelter

Shelter Constructed ☐

Type of Shelter

Clothing/Coverings ☐

Waterproof ☐

Animal proof ☐

Sunproof ☐

Fire Started ☐

Food Inventory

Rations ☐

Water ☐

Hunting ☐

Fishing ☐

Foraging ☐

Journey

Distance Covered

Trail Markers Used

Landmarks Sighted

Animal Prints

Map Sketch

Lat.

Long.

Party Member	Status	Injuries	Treatment

Date ______________

Conditions

Weather

Terrain

Shelter

Shelter Constructed ☐

Type of Shelter

Clothing/Coverings ☐

Waterproof ☐

Animal proof ☐

Sunproof ☐

Fire Started ☐

Food Inventory

Rations ☐

Water ☐

Hunting ☐

Fishing ☐

Foraging ☐

Journey

Distance Covered

Trail Markers Used

Landmarks Sighted

Animal Prints

Map Sketch

Lat. Long.

Party Member	Status	Injuries	Treatment

Date ____________

Conditions

Weather

Terrain

Food Inventory

Rations ☐

Water ☐

Hunting ☐

Fishing ☐

Foraging ☐

Journey

Distance Covered

Trail Markers Used

Landmarks Sighted

Animal Prints

Shelter

Shelter Constructed ☐

Type of Shelter

Clothing/Coverings ☐

Waterproof ☐

Animal proof ☐

Sunproof ☐

Fire Started ☐

Map Sketch

Lat. Long.

Party Member	Status	Injuries	Treatment

Date

Conditions

Weather

Terrain

Shelter

Shelter Constructed ☐

Type of Shelter

Clothing/Coverings ☐

Waterproof ☐

Animal proof ☐

Sunproof ☐

Fire Started ☐

Food Inventory

Rations ☐

Water ☐

Hunting ☐

Fishing ☐

Foraging ☐

Journey

Distance Covered

Trail Markers Used

Landmarks Sighted

Animal Prints

Map Sketch

Lat. Long.

Party Member	Status	Injuries	Treatment

Date

Conditions

Weather

Terrain

Shelter

Shelter Constructed ☐

Type of Shelter

Clothing/Coverings ☐

Waterproof ☐

Animal proof ☐

Sunproof ☐

Fire Started ☐

Food Inventory

Rations ☐

Water ☐

Hunting ☐

Fishing ☐

Foraging ☐

Journey

Distance Covered

Trail Markers Used

Landmarks Sighted

Animal Prints

Map Sketch

Lat. Long.

Party Member	Status	Injuries	Treatment

Date

Conditions

Weather

Terrain

Shelter

Shelter Constructed ☐

Type of Shelter

Clothing/Coverings ☐

Waterproof ☐

Animal proof ☐

Sunproof ☐

Fire Started ☐

Food Inventory

Rations ☐

Water ☐

Hunting ☐

Fishing ☐

Foraging ☐

Journey

Distance Covered

Trail Markers Used

Landmarks Sighted

Animal Prints

Map Sketch

Lat.

Long.

Party Member	Status	Injuries	Treatment

Date

Conditions

Weather

Terrain

Food Inventory

Rations ☐

Water ☐

Hunting ☐

Fishing ☐

Foraging ☐

Journey

Distance Covered

Trail Markers Used

Landmarks Sighted

Animal Prints

Shelter

Shelter Constructed ☐

Type of Shelter

Clothing/Coverings ☐

Waterproof ☐

Animal proof ☐

Sunproof ☐

Fire Started ☐

Map Sketch

Lat. Long.

Party Member	Status	Injuries	Treatment

Date ______________

Conditions

Weather

Terrain

Food Inventory

Rations ☐

Water ☐

Hunting ☐

Fishing ☐

Foraging ☐

Journey

Distance Covered

Trail Markers Used

Landmarks Sighted

Animal Prints

Shelter

Shelter Constructed ☐

Type of Shelter

Clothing/Coverings ☐

Waterproof ☐

Animal proof ☐

Sunproof ☐

Fire Started ☐

Map Sketch

Lat. Long.

Party Member	Status	Injuries	Treatment

Date ____________

Conditions

Weather

Terrain

Shelter

Shelter Constructed ☐

Type of Shelter

Clothing/Coverings ☐

Waterproof ☐

Animal proof ☐

Sunproof ☐

Fire Started ☐

Food Inventory

Rations ☐

Water ☐

Hunting ☐

Fishing ☐

Foraging ☐

Journey

Distance Covered

Trail Markers Used

Landmarks Sighted

Animal Prints

Map Sketch

Lat. Long.

Party Member	Status	Injuries	Treatment

Date ____________

Conditions

Weather

Terrain

Shelter

Shelter Constructed ☐

Type of Shelter

Clothing/Coverings ☐

Waterproof ☐

Animal proof ☐

Sunproof ☐

Fire Started ☐

Food Inventory

Rations ☐

Water ☐

Hunting ☐

Fishing ☐

Foraging ☐

Journey

Distance Covered

Trail Markers Used

Landmarks Sighted

Animal Prints

Map Sketch

Lat.

Long.

Party Member	Status	Injuries	Treatment

www.ingramcontent.com/pod-product-compliance
Lightning Source LLC
LaVergne TN
LVHW060138080526
838202LV00049B/4017
* 9 7 8 3 3 4 7 0 2 9 7 0 5 *